Bilingual
Guide
to Japan

·

BUDDHIST STATUARY

ISHII Ayako

Illustrated by IWASAKI Jun

SHOGAKUKAN

Bilingual Guide to Japan
BUDDHIST STATUARY

ISHII Ayako
Illustrated by IWASAKI Jun

Book and Cover design © Kindaichi Design
English translation © Lingua Guild

Published by
SHOGAKUKAN
2-3-1 Hitotsubashi Chiyoda-Ku,
Tokyo 101-8001 JAPAN
http://www.shogakukan.co.jp

This book is a new edition of BUTSUZŌ ZUKAI SHINSHO
published by SHOGAKUKAN in 2010,
with extensive additions and modification.

BUTSUZŌ BILINGUAL GUIDE by
ISHII Ayako, IWASAKI Jun
© 2016 ISHII Ayako, IWASAKI Jun ╱ SHOGAKUKAN
Printed in Japan
ISBN 978-4-09-388460-0

仏像バイリンガルガイド

石井亜矢子

岩﨑 隼 画

小学館

English Renderings of Buddhist Terms

This English and Japanese bilingual book introduces the representative types of Buddhist statues found in Japan and explains how the different types can be distinguished.

● All Japanese terms are rendered in italicized Roman characters. The only diacritical marks used are the macron (ˉ), to indicate long vowel sounds, and the hyphen (-), to separate two adjacent long vowel sounds.

Example: 不動明王 is rendered as ***Fudō Myō-ō***.

● All Sanskrit terms are rendered in Roman characters. In some cases, phonetic symbols have been omitted. Equivalent English translations are provided next to the Sanskrit.

Example: 薬師如来 is rendered as ***Yakushi Nyorai*** (Bhaiṣajyaguru: Medicine Buddha).

              ↑   ↑   ↑

Romanized Japanese term (in italics)

Romanized Sanskrit term

English translation

Since the conventions for rendering these terms into English differ depending on the facility (temple, shrine, or public institute, etc.), terms used elsewhere may not be consistent with those used in this book. Given that even Japanese names and pronunciations of Buddhist statues may differ depending on the sect or region, they cannot be generalized. Standard names are used in this book and are rendered so that they can be easily read by individuals who are not native speakers of Japanese.

本書の英文表記について

●日本語はすべてローマ字読みにし、斜体のアルファベットで表記しています。発音記号は長音記号マクロン (ˉ) のみ表記し、母音が続き発音しにくい場合はハイフン (−) を使用しています。

〈例〉不動明王　***Fudō Myō-ō***

●サンスクリット語はすべてローマ字読みにし、アルファベットで表記しています。発音記号は省略している場合もあります。同意の英語訳も並記しています。

〈例〉薬師如来　***Yakushi Nyorai*** (Bhaiṣajyaguru : Medicine Buddha)

         ↑   ↑   ↑

日本名のローマ字表記(斜字)　サンスクリット名のローマ字表記　英訳

※これら外国語表記は、施設 (寺社や美術館、公共施設等) ごとに異なるルールで表記されているため、本書と一致しない場合があります。特に仏像の名称とその発音については、宗派や地方によって日本語でも呼び方が異なることがあり、一般化はできません。本書では標準的な呼称を掲載し、外国語を母語とする読者ができるだけ平易に発音できる表記としました。

Table of Contents 目次

Introduction

The teachings of Buddha, who was also known as Shākyamuni or Siddhārtha Gautama, gave birth to Buddhism in the 6th and 5th centuries BCE. Five hundred years after Shākyamuni's death, the first Buddhist statues were sculpted in his image at Gandhara (present-day Pakistan) and Mathura (Uttar Pradesh, Northern India). With the flowering of Mahayana Buddhism, not only images of Buddha but also three-dimensional representations of *bosatsu* (bodhisattva) and *myō-ō* (vidyārāja), which in Japanese are called *butsuzō*, became increasingly common.

Buddhism and *butsuzō* first made their way from India to Japan via the Korean Peninsula in the mid-6th century CE. Since then, Buddhism has been transmitted to every corner of the land. One finds temples and worship halls in every part of the country, and the numerous statues enshrined in these places of worship bear witness to the fact that prayers continue to be offered to Buddha.

There are various types of *butsuzō*, each given a different role by Shākyamuni. To properly fulfill these roles, each type of statue is given a specific countenance and physical carriage. The characteristics and profile given to a *butsuzō* contain the Buddha's teachings, and at the same time, the wishes and devotion of the people are carved into its image.

はじめに

　紀元前6〜5世紀ごろに、北インドに生まれたゴータマ・シッダールタ（釈迦）によって、仏教は誕生した。釈迦が没し約500年を経て、ガンダーラ（現パキスタン）やマトゥラー（インド北部）で釈迦が初めて刻まれた。仏像の誕生である。以後、大乗仏教の発展にともない、釈迦の姿だけでなく、菩薩や明王など、つくられる仏像の種類も増えていった。

　インドから遠く離れた日本の地に、朝鮮半島を経由して仏教と仏像がもたらされたのは、6世紀半ばのこと。以後、仏教は日本のすみずみにまで伝播。どんな土地にも寺院やお堂が建つ。そのありようを示す証人のひとつが、各地にのこされている仏像である。

　仏像には、さまざまな種類がある。それは、釈迦から与えられた役割がそれぞれ違うから。仏像はその与えられた役目を果たすため、それにふさわしい表情や身体の特徴を

Proper Conduct at Temples

Butsuzō are not to be appreciated, they are to be worshipped. One should always keep this in mind when visiting a temple and its statues. Wherever a *butsuzō* is enshrined, there will always be people there who have come to express their devotion and offer their prayers. This is the same at small, unattended Buddha halls and at great temple complexes; these are places of faith dedicated to protecting the Buddha who, in turn, gives them protection. This should not be forgotten. It is important to conduct oneself properly and to do one's best not to offend anyone.

For example, at temples that do not require visitor admission fees, if dress is too casual (shorts and rubber sandals, etc.) a person may be denied entrance because their purpose for entering the premises is not seen to be for worship. Once inside a temple, hats or head coverings should be removed, and when approaching a *butsuzō,* it is best to do so with your palms together. Whether a practicing Buddhist or not, one should show gratitude for the opportunity to visit the temple, and it is proper to greet the Buddha with this attitude.

To enshrine a particular statue means that a Buddhist world centered on that Buddha is being created. A temple spares no effort for its *butsuzō*, whether it is the architecture or the attention to detail in the smallest utensils and paraphernalia. A temple is a

もつ。それぞれの仏像には、釈迦の教えが込められていると同時に、仏像を欲した人々の願いや信仰のかたちが刻まれている。

拝観の心得

　仏像は見るものではなく、拝むもの。寺院で仏を拝観する場合は、このことを意識する必要がある。仏像が祀られている場には、お参りに来られるかたがかならずいる。それは無住の小さなお堂でも、著名な大寺院でも変わりはない。仏を護り、守られる暮らしの現場であることを忘れずに、失礼にならないように心がけることが大切だ。

　たとえば、拝観料を定めていないような寺院では、短パンにゴム草履というような、くだけすぎた服装では、礼拝目的とみなされず、拝観を断られる場合があるのでご注意を。堂内

temple is a manifestation of a universe. *Butsuzō*, when housed in an art gallery or museum, may be rendered a piece of sculpture. By contrast, a temple is a place consecrated for the Buddha, so the essential experience of a "visit" is gained when one takes in the entire sanctified space and atmosphere dedicated to the Buddha.

Most temples prohibit photography inside the worship halls. Because the space is set-aside for quiet prayer, the use of mobile phones and other electronic devices and flashlights are restricted. When asking to visit, it is assumed that the visitor will obey the instructions and rules established by the temple. There are temples that are quite strict in this respect, but we hope you can accommodate these restrictions as part of the enjoyment of your visit.

では帽子をとり、仏像に手を合わせていただきたい。仏教徒であるかどうかにかかわらず、この場所に来ることができた感謝の意味を込めて、仏様に挨拶していただきたいと思う。

仏像を安置するということは、その仏を中心とする仏教世界をつくるということ。寺院は、その建築から小さな荘厳具にいたるまで、すべて仏のために限りを尽くし、この世に現出させたひとつの宇宙といえる。仏像は、美術館や博物館では、ともすれば「彫刻」となってしまう。寺院という仏のためにつくられた空間で向き合い、寺院の佇まいとともに味わうことが、「拝観」の醍醐味である。

ほとんどの寺院では、堂内の撮影を禁止している。静寂な祈りの空間であるため、携帯電話などの電子機器や、懐中電灯の使用も制限されている。拝観を乞うということは、そのお寺の決まりに従うということ。厳格な約束ごとも含めて楽しんでいただきたい。

Chapter 1

Basic Knowledge of Buddhist Statuary

第一章

仏像の基本

Types of *Butsuzō*

Butsuzō, Buddhist statuary, is classified and ranked into four major groups: **nyorai** (tathāgata), **bosatsu** (bodhisattva), **myō-ō** (vidyārāja), and **ten** (deva). This hierarchy does not designate value to these beings, but simply distinguishes them according to the roles they play in the Buddhist pantheon.

Butsuzō may, at times, be positioned on an altar by itself, but in most cases they are enshrined with several others. The *honzon* is the *butsuzō* that is the central focus of worship at each temple. The basic arrangement is a triad with one statue positioned in the middle (*chūson*), and two statues positioned on its flanks that act as assistants (*wakiji*). Any statue from any one of the four major groups can be located in the *chūson* position, but seldom are statues in a superior group assigned the *wakiji* positions to a *chuson* from an inferior group. For example, if a *nyorai* is in the central position, then *bosatsu*, who are still striving to become *nyorai*, will be designated the flanking positions, and deities from the *ten* group will be positioned to form a protective perimeter around the triad.

仏像の種類

　仏像は、「如来・菩薩・明王・天」の4部に大別することができる。筆頭は如来で、以下順番に格が下がっていく。しかしこのヒエラルキーは、仏の価値とはまったく関係せず、役割に応じた区別にすぎない。

　仏像は単独で安置される場合もあるが、複数の仏が同時に祀られることが多い。本尊とは各寺で礼拝の中心となる仏のことで、一尊を中央にすえて、その中尊を助ける二尊が両脇を固め脇侍となる「三尊形式」が基本のかたち。このとき、どのグループの仏でも中尊になれるが、中尊より格上グループの仏が脇侍になることは、ほとんどない。たとえば、如来が中尊の場合、如来を目指す立場の菩薩が脇侍となり、菩薩より格下の天グループの仏が周囲を固め、三尊を護るのである。

These arrangements illustrate the relationships between the groups in the Buddhist pantheon, and should be understood not as designating hierarchy, but rather as indicating the stage of being each group is at. This serves to complement the relationships they have with each other.

It should be noted that the *myō-ō* are sometimes not discussed in terms of this hierarchy. The reason is that the idea of *myō-ō* appeared out of esoteric Buddhism that evolved in the final period of Buddhism's development in India. Therefore, the *myō-ō* are based on a very different way of thinking, and were introduced at a time when the relationships among the *nyorai, bosatsu,* and *ten* were already well established.

On the following pages are examples of how the four groups relate to each other.

これが仏教におけるグループの関係性で、決して上下関係ではなく、お互いがお互いの立場を理解し、補完し合う間柄といえる。

ちなみに明王は、このヒエラルキーで語るにはなじまない仏である。というのも、明王はインドにおける仏教の最終展開である密教の尊格。如来と菩薩、それを護る天部という関係が成立していたなかに、遅れて加わった異なる考え方の存在であるからだ。

次のページから、各グループの関係性を示す例をみていただこう。

Yakushi Triad

Gakkō Bosatsu
(Candraprabha: Moonlight bodhisattva)
月光菩薩

Yakushi Nyorai
(Bhaiṣajyaguru: Medicine Buddha)
薬師如来

The central *chūson* is *Yakushi Nyorai* (p. 26), who is flanked on the left by *Nikkō Bosatsu* and on the right by *Gakkō Bosatsu*. The triad arrangement is the basic format for enshrining *butsuzō*. As shown on the next two pages, deities stand guard in the directions of north, south, east, and west to protect the triad. This role is predominantly reserved for deities from the *ten* group.

Nikkō Bosatsu
(Sūryaprabha: Sunlight bodhisattva)
にっこう ぼ さつ
日光菩薩

やく し さんぞん
薬師三尊
ちゅうそん
　中尊が薬師如来（p.26）、左脇（向
かって右）に立つのが日光菩薩、右
脇（向かって左）に立つのが月光菩
薩。これを三尊形式といい、仏像を
安置する基本パターンとなっている。
まち
その三尊の四隅を護るのが、次の見
けんぞく
開きページで紹介する眷属で、主と
てん ぶ
して天部の仏がその役割を担う。

13

Shitennō Tetrad

The *Shitennō* (p. 80) combination is commonly found serving *nyorai* and *bosatsu* by standing guard in the four directions. They are from the *ten* group of deities. At times, only two of the four statues appear, mostly as pairs of *Jikokuten* and *Zōchōten* or of *Kōmokuten* and *Tamonten*.

Kōmokuten
(Virūpākṣa: West)
こうもくてん
広目天 (西)

Zōchōten
(Virūḍhaka: South)
ぞうちょうてん
増長天 (南)

四天王（p.80）は、ほとんどの如来・菩薩に仕えてその四方を護る、いわばオールマイティの天部チーム。持国天と増長天、広目天と多聞天がペアを組む二天の場合もある。

Tamonten
(Vaiśravana: North)

多聞天（北）

Jikokuten
(Dhṛtarāṣṭra: East)

持国天（東）

Godai Myō-ō Pentad

The *myō-ō* are part of the esoteric Buddhist pantheon. Of these, the most supreme is *Fudō Myō-ō* (p. 58), who is often found surrounded by the four other deities in a powerful combination known as *Godai Myō-ō* (p. 60).

Daiitoku Myō-ō
(Yamāntaka: West)
だい い とく みょうおう
大威徳明王 (西)

Gundari Myō-ō
(Kuṇḍalī: South)
ぐん だ り みょうおう
軍荼利明王 (南)

Kongōyasha Myō-ō
(Vajrayakṣa: North)
こんごうやしゃみょうおう
金剛夜叉明王（北）

五大明王
ごだいみょうおう

　明王は、密教の仏。そのなかでも最高の存在である不動明王（p.58）を中心に、四明王が取り囲む五大明王（p.60）は、最高に強力な群像。

Gōzanze Myō-ō
(Trilokavijaya: East)
こうざんぜみょうおう
降三世明王（東）

Fudo Myō-ō
(Acalanátha: Immovable One)
ふどうみょうおう
不動明王

Materials used for Buddhist Statues

The first Buddhist statues were brought to Japan in the 6th century and are thought to have been *kondōbutsu* (gilded bronze statues) that were made in the Korean Peninsula. Later, during the *Nara* period (8th century), *sozō* (clay) and *kanshitsuzō* (dry lacquer technique using hemp cloth soaked and layered with lacquer) statues brought from China became popular.

In Japan, however, wood carving became the mainstay technique of making Buddhist statuary. This was because Japan is a country blessed with rich forests, so wood was the most convenient material to work with and the Japanese were already familiar with and skilled at woodwork. Initially, the *ichibokuzukuri* (single block sculpting) technique was employed to carve the main torso and head portion of a statue from one solid piece of wood. By the early *Heian* period (late 8th–9th century) this method of carving had become highly developed, and many unique and attractive *butsuzō* were being produced.

仏像の材質

　日本に仏像が初めてもたらされたのは、6世紀のこと。朝鮮半島で制作された金銅仏だったと考えられる。その後、奈良時代（8世紀）には中国から伝えられた粘土づくりの塑像、麻布を漆で貼り固める乾漆像が流行した。しかし、日本で主流となったのは、木彫像だった。日本は豊かな森林に恵まれた国であり、日本人にとってはもっとも入手しやすく、加工にもなれていた素材が木だったのである。

　一本の木材でつくる「一木造り」は、体躯の根幹部分を一材で彫りだすもの。平安時代初期（8世紀後半〜9世紀）には彫技も高まり、多くの個性的かつ魅力的な仏像が生みだされた。

In the middle of the *Heian* period (11th century), the master statue carver *Jōchō* (p. 111) perfected the *yosegizukuri* (joined block sculpting) technique, and since then this has become a common method for making Buddhist statuary. Although most *butsuzō* made in the 21st century are made with the *yosegizukuri* technique, other carving methods are also used, especially in cases when reverence is being shown to a particularly sacred tree.

平安時代中期 (11世紀) に、仏師 (p.106) の定朝 (p.111) によって、複数の材を組み合わせる「寄木造り」が完成されると、その後はこの技法が主流となった。21世紀につくられる仏像の多くも寄木造りだが、特定の木に対する信仰がある場合は、現代においてもその限りではない。

Chapter 2

Nyorai Statuary

第二章

如来部の仏像

The Tathāgata Statues: *Butsuzō* of *Nyorai*

The literal meaning of the Sanskrit term tathāgata (*nyorai* in Japanese) is "one who has thus come from the truth." It is the highest title given to one whom, after enduring rigorous training and practice, has attained enlightenment.

In Gandhara, the hair of *nyorai* statues had been sculpted in waves, but in Japan, it is traditional to carve it in small, tightly bound, clamshell knots called *rahotsu*. On top of the head is a small hemisphere where the skull is swelled or raised up. This raised portion is thought to contain wisdom. The peculiar shape of the skull and the hair in the *rahotsu* style are defining characteristics of *nyorai* statues that are not found on any other type of *butsuzō*.

In general, the body is covered with only two pieces of cloth; a wrap-around, skirt-like cloth (*mo*) covers the lower body and a 10-meter-long stole (*kesa*) covers the upper body. It has no decorative jewelry or accessories and has a very simple appearance. This simplicity represents the story of Shākyamuni who, when becoming an ascetic, threw away all attachment to this world. *Butsuzō* of *nyorai* are the simplest representations of the highest possible form of invocation.

如来部の仏像

　如来というサンスクリット語の直訳は、「真実から来た者」。厳しい修行を積んで悟りを開いた、仏の称号のなかでも最高のものだ。

　ガンダーラでは波打つ髪だった如来の頭髪は、日本では螺髪という、貝殻状の小さな髪束で覆われる。頭頂部は盛り上がっており、この盛り上がり部分は、知恵のかたまりだといわれている。この頭のかたちと螺髪が、他の仏にはない如来の目印である。

　身に着けるのは、通常は2枚の布のみ。1枚は、腰に巻きつけて下半身を覆う裳というもの。もう1枚は、上半身から下半身までを覆う10メートルほどの長い袈裟という長い布である。装身具の類も一切身に着けることなく、簡素な姿をしている。これは、釈迦が出家するとき、すべての執着を捨てたことに由来しているという。シンプルな造形に無上の存在を込めたのが、如来という仏像である。

Shaka Nyorai
(Shākyamuni: Buddha)

Shaka Nyorai is the origin of all Buddhist statuary and is considered the pinnacle of the *nyorai* group. The first orthodox temple built in Japan was *Asukadera* Temple (present-day *Angoin* Temple, *Nara*), where the *honzon*, *Asuka Daibutsu*, is of *Shaka Nyorai*. Many *Shaka Nyorai* statues are holding the palm-up *semui-in* mudra (see *Inzō*, p. 110) and the palm-down *yogan-in* mudra, which together mean that "everything is alright and a wish will be fulfilled." Although *Shaka Nyorai* statues are often seated or standing, there are other variations that represent events in Shākayamuni's life such as the pose of Shākyamuni at his birth (see *Tanjōbutsu*, p. 116) and at his passing away (see *Nehan*, p. 113). These statues express a deep respect and memorialization of Shākyamuni as a real person. Perhaps the most pronounced form of this is the standing *Shaka Nyorai* at *Seiryōji* Temple (*Kyoto*), which contains the "five vital organs" made of silk.

釈迦如来

　すべての仏像の原点であり、如来グループの筆頭である。日本に初めてつくられた本格的な寺院、飛鳥寺(現安居院、奈良)の「飛鳥大仏」と呼ばれる本尊も釈迦如来だった。釈迦如来の多くは、掌を前に向けて上げる施無畏印と、下げる与願印という印相(p.110)を結び、「大丈夫、願いをかなえる」ことをあらわす。多くは坐像か立像だが、釈迦如来にはさらにバリエーションがある。生まれたときは誕生仏(p.116)として、没する状況は涅槃像(p.113)として、その生涯のさまざまな場面が釈迦像としてつくられているのだ。これは、実在の人物である釈迦に対する深い敬意と追慕にほかならない。究極といえるのが、清凉寺(京都)の釈迦如来立像で、絹でつくった「五臓」が像内に納められている。

Yakushi Nyorai
(Bhaiṣajyaguru: Medicine Buddha)

The realms the *nyorai* and *bosatsu* inhabit are called *jōdo* (pure lands). *Yakushi Nyorai* resides in the *rurikōjōdo* (Eastern lapis lazuli pure land) from where he offers help to believers suffering from hardships such as sickness and poverty that can strike anyone. As a rule, *nyorai* statues do not hold anything in their hands. However, an exception is found with the *Yakushi Nyorai* that are thought to help in recovering from illness when worshiped, which carry *yakko* (medicine jars). In many cases, *Yakushi Nyorai* are positioned between *Nikkō Bosatsu* and *Gakkō Bosatsu* (p. 12), as seen at *Yakushiji* Temple (*Nara*, p. 118), and it is not rare to find a group of *Jūnishinshō* (p. 86) in accompaniment. During times of natural disasters or frequent political upheaval, such as in 8th and 9th century Japan, *Yakushi Nyorai* statues attract great devotion because they offer salvation from national calamities and social unrest. In esoteric Buddhism, *Yakushi Nyorai* was the *honzon* used in the process of exorcising malicious spirits. *Yakushi Nyorai* statues are given different features compared with other *butsuzō* because of the various types of supplications laid before them.

薬師如来

　　如来・菩薩の住まいを浄土というが、薬師如来は東方の瑠璃光浄土に住まい、病や貧困など人々に起こりえる災厄に寄り添う。特に病気平癒に利益があり、何も持たないのが原則である如来のなかで、例外的に薬壺を手にすることが多い。薬師寺（奈良、p.119）のように日光・月光菩薩を従え三尊として祀られる例が多く（p.12)、さらに十二神将（p.86）を従える場合も少なくない。8〜9世紀の薬師像には天変地異や政変など、国家的な社会不安からの救済が託され、密教では怨霊調伏などの修法の本尊となっていた。他の仏像に比べて容貌に違いがあるのは、託された願いが異なるからなのかもしれない。

Amida Nyorai
(Amitābha: Buddha of Infinite Light)

If one recites the chant "*Namu Amida Butsu*" and accumulates merit, *Amida Nyorai* will come to receive the person at death to go and be reborn in *gokurakujōdo* (blissful pure land). *Namu* expresses devotion and praise, so the chant means "Oh, wonderful *Amida*." People entrust *Amida Nyorai* with their happiness, not in this world, but in the next. The peaceful *Amida Nyorai* made by *Jōchō*, which is now seated in *Byōdōin* Temple (*Kyoto*, p. 119), was considered the highest *butsuzō* to offer vows of devotion to among the nobility in the 11th century. *Amida Nyorai* statues are often arranged together in a triad with *bosatsu*. A famous triad of this grouping carved by *Kaikei* (p. 111), which can be found at *Jōdoji* Temple (*Hyogo*), captures the moment when the triad meets a devotee in the next world.

阿弥陀如来

「南無阿弥陀仏」と唱えて功徳を積めば、臨終の折に阿弥陀如来が迎えに来て、その住まいである極楽浄土に往生できる。生きている間ではなく、死後の世界での幸福を、人々はこの仏に託した。「南無」とは、帰依する思いをあらわす言葉。意訳すれば、「阿弥陀さま、素敵！」ということになる。11世紀の貴族には、定朝の造立した円満な容貌の平等院（京都、p.119）の阿弥陀如来坐像が、帰依を誓う最上の仏であった。阿弥陀如来は菩薩を従え、三尊像としてつくられることが多い。来迎の様子をあらわす影像では、快慶（p.111）の手になる浄土寺（兵庫）の三尊が知られる。

Dainichi Nyorai

(Mahāvairocana)

Dainichi Nyorai is the highest manifestation in esoteric Buddhism. *Dainichi Nyorai* rules the two worlds of truth and wisdom, which are represented as the realms of *taizōkai* and *kongōkai*. Esoteric Buddhism considers all buddhas, including *Shaka Nyorai*, as incarnations or embodiments of *Dainichi Nyorai*. This cosmology is represented in mandalas (p. 113). *Dainichi Nyorai* statues appear as if they were *bosatsu* with long bound hair and wearing various adornments. Unlike *bosatsu*, however, these statues do not stand but are always seated in the lotus position known as *kekkafuza*. As shown in the illustration, many of the *Kongōkai Dainichi Nyorai* statues form the *chiken-in* mudra, which symbolizes deep wisdom. This is a powerful mudra which concentrates all energy. It is often difficult to distinguish statues by their mudras alone, but if it is forming *chiken-in*, then there is no mistake it is *Dainichi Nyorai*. The rare *Taizōkai Dainichi Nyorai* statues form the *zenjō-in* mudra.

大日如来

　　密教世界の中心に存在する最高の仏。道理と智慧のふたつの世界、胎蔵界と金剛界を治める。密教では、釈迦如来も含めたすべての仏は、大日如来の化身と考える。その世界観を示したものが曼荼羅（p.113）である。長い髪を結い上げ、装身具で身を飾る姿は、まるで菩薩。しかし、菩薩のように立像は存在せず、かならず両足を交差して重ねる結跏趺坐という姿で座っている。イラストのように智拳印を結ぶ金剛界の大日如来像が数多くつくられているが、智拳印とは智慧の深さを象徴し、力をすべてここに集中させるという強いもの。印相だけで尊名を見分けることは難しいが、智拳印を結んでいれば大日如来に間違いない。仏像としては作例は少ないが、胎蔵界の大日如来像は、禅定印を結んでいる。

Trivia

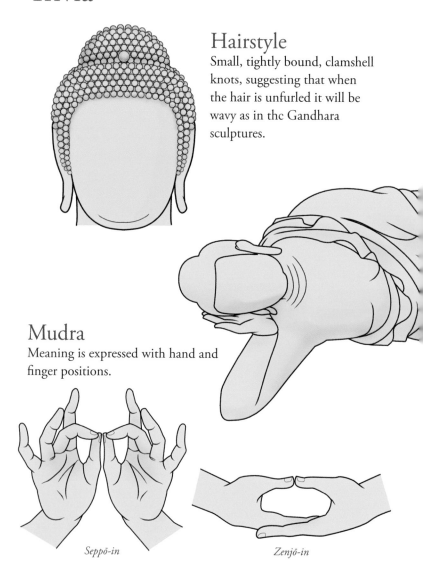

Hairstyle
Small, tightly bound, clamshell knots, suggesting that when the hair is unfurled it will be wavy as in the Gandhara sculptures.

Mudra
Meaning is expressed with hand and finger positions.

Seppō-in

Zenjō-in

Hands and Feet

Shaka Nyorai is revered for body features which no other human possesses. Webbed fingers and toes will save all sentient beings without letting anyone fall through.

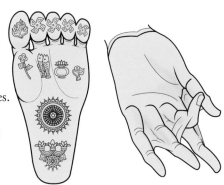

Lying on the Side

The nirvana pose expresses the attainment of total liberation.

●豆知識

髪型

貝殻にように巻かれた小さな髪束は、まるでカーラーを巻いたよう。ほどけばガンダーラ仏のようなウエーブになるかも。

印相（説法印、禅定印）

手指のかたちは、仏の意思をあらわす。

手足

釈迦如来には、人間にはない尊い身体的特徴がある。指の間の水かきは、衆生を漏れなく救うことのあらわれ。

横臥

解脱の境地に至ったことを意味するもので、涅槃と呼ばれる。

Chapter *3*

Bosatsu Statuary

第三章

菩薩部の仏像

The Bodhisattva Statues: *Butsuzō* of *Bosatsu*

The literal meaning of the Sanskrit term bodhisattva (*bosatu* in Japanese) is "one in search of enlightenment." To become *nyorai*, these beings persevere in rigorous practice. However, they are not doing this for themselves; they have taken a vow to save all sentient beings through their practice. With strong determination they have chosen to stay close to sentient beings. Although only one step away from enlightenment, the *bosatsu* are filled with benevolence and a commitment to bring salvation to all living souls.

Butsuzō of *bosatsu* are modeled on the princely appearance of Shākyamuni before he left his home. Because these statues are adorned in the way the nobility clothed themselves in ancient India, their dress is luxurious. Their long, straight hair is tied up and decorated with crowns, and they wear decorative accessories such as necklaces, bracelets, and earrings. Below the waist they wear gorgeous, full cloth skirting called *mo* or *kun*, and diagonally across the shoulder is draped a long piece of cloth called a *jōhaku*. Another shawl called a *tenne* flows over the shoulders and arms. In addition to the soft, kind facial countenance of *bosatsu* statues, the exposed torso also allows one to appreciate their physicality.

菩薩部の仏像

　サンスクリット語の意味は、悟りを求める者。如来となるために、修行に励んでいるとされる存在だ。しかしそれは、自らのためだけではない。すべての人々を救済するという誓願をたて、修行しているのである。あえて衆生のそばにて、誰をも等しく救ってくれる慈悲の仏なのだ。

　その姿は、出家する以前の王子時代の釈迦がモデル。古代インドの貴族の正装であるため、たいへん豪華だ。長く伸ばしたまっすぐな髪を結い上げて冠で飾り、ネックレスやブレスレット、イヤリングなどで着飾っている。下半身には裳または裙という大型の布を巻き、上半身は条帛という長い布を肩から斜めに掛け、両肩や腕にはショールのような天衣という細長い布をまとう。上半身の露出度が高く、肉体の様子がうかがえるところが、優しい表情とともに、菩薩という仏像の大きな見どころとなっている。

Miroku Bosatsu

(Maitreya)

Appearing 5.67 billion years after Shākyamuni's death, *Miroku Bosatsu* will descend to this world offering salvation to all humans. Shākyamuni promised that *Miroku Bosatsu* would be elevated to *nyorai*, and for this reason, statues can be found depicting *Miroku* not only as a *bosatsu,* but also in a small number of cases, as a *nyorai*. A striking feature of many *Miroku Bosatsu* statues is their *hankashiyuizō* position, in which they sit half-lotus on a chair with the right leg resting across the left thigh, and their right hand lightly touching the right cheek. This position represents the deep meditative state entered on the way to save those who have slipped through the net of Shākyamuni's salvation. The two most famous statues which hold this pose are found at *Kōryūji* Temple (*Kyoto*, p. 120) and *Chūgūji* Temple (*Nara*, p. 120). Both date from the 7th century and are carved from wood. After the 7th century, the number of statues produced with this pose decreased rapidly and were replaced with variations that were either standing with a lotus flower and water jar (see *Jimotsu*, p. 110) or seated with hands folded in the *zenjō-in* mudra with a pagoda resting on their palms. *Daigoji* Temple (*Kyoto*) houses an excellent example of the latter, which was made by *Kaikei* at the end of the 12th century.

弥勒菩薩

　釈迦の入滅から56億7000万年後、この世に降り立って人々を救う。釈迦によって、如来となることが菩薩時代から約束されていたため、菩薩だけでなく、数は少ないが弥勒如来もつくられている。印象的な弥勒菩薩は、椅子に足を組んで腰掛け、右手を軽く頬にあてる半跏思惟像。釈迦の救いから漏れた人々を、どうすれば救えるのかと瞑想にふける姿だ。このポーズで名高いのが、広隆寺（京都、p.121）と中宮寺（奈良、p.121）の2像。いずれも7世紀の木彫像である。以降は、半跏思惟像は激減。水瓶（p.110　持物）をのせた蓮華を持つ立像や、禅定印を結んだ手の上に宝塔をのせる坐像が主流となる。醍醐寺（京都）には、12世紀に快慶がつくった端正な坐像が祀られている。

Shō Kannon
(Āryāvalokiteśvara)

Kannon was born in 1st-century India. Among the *bosatsu* statuary this deity has the most variations. According to Buddhist scriptures, *Kannon* offers salvation to all sentient beings and is believed to have thirty-three manifestations. For this reason, many types of *Kannon* statues have been created. These are collectively referred to as *Henge* (transformed) *Kannon*. *Shō Kannon* is the basic appearance and so it has one face and two arms. Old examples of the thirty-three manifestations are the *Kuse Kannon* at *Hōryūji* Temple (*Nara*, p. 120), which holds a *hōju* (wish-granting jewel), and the statue in *Tōindō* Hall at *Yakushiji* Temple (*Nara*), whose hands are in the *semui-in* and *yogan-in* mudras. There are many other *Kannon* statues representing the other manifestations. One feature that makes a statue identifiable as a *Kannon* is the jeweled crown which features *kebutsu*, a small figure representing the original incarnation of *Amida Nyorai*. The *Kudara Kannon* at *Hōryūji* Temple was finally identified as a *Kannon* when its crown was discovered to have a *kebutsu*.

聖観音

　紀元1世紀ころにインドで誕生した観音は、菩薩グループのなかで、もっともバリエーションが多い。33に身を変え、衆生を救うと経典に説かれることから、多数の観音が生みだされた。それを変化観音というが、聖観音は変化する前。いわば観音の基本形で、顔はひとつで腕は2本である。古くは、法隆寺（奈良、p.121）の救世観音のように両手で災いを除き、願いをかなえてくれる宝珠を持つ像、薬師寺（奈良）東院堂像のように持物をとらずに施無畏・与願印を結ぶ像など、さまざまな像容の観音像がつくられた。聖観音に限らず、阿弥陀如来の化仏のついた宝冠は観音の目印。化仏は姿を変える前の姿を示し、宝冠が発見されたことで観音と判明したのが、法隆寺の百済観音像である。

Jūichimen Kannon
(Ekādaśamukha)

The shapes of *Kannon* statues depict the roles the deities play and the meritorious deeds they perform. A good example is the *Jūichimen Kannon* which are characterized by the presence of many small faces attached to the top of the main head. This shows that the *Jūichimen Kannon* are looking in every direction and can see the suffering of all people. Some of the faces are calm and benign, while others show rage or laughter. Two *Jūichimen Kannon* are enshrined in *Nigatsudō* Hall at *Tōdaiji* Temple (*Nara*). During the *Omizutori* ceremony, penitence is made to these *hibutsu* (p. 109) for the sins of all humankind and prayers are offered asking for peace over the land. The *honzon* at *Hasedera* Temple (*Nara*) is renowned for being particularly propitious. In general, *Jūichimen Kannon* stand on lotus dais (see *Daiza,* p. 107) holding lotus flowers or water jars, but the statue at *Hasedera* Temple sits on a base that is shaped like a stone and holds a *shakujō* (monk's staff).

じゅういちめんかんのん
十一面観音

　姿を変えて働く観音には、自らがもつ役割や利益を、目にみえるかたちで示すものがある。代表的なのが、頭上に小さな顔をのせたこの仏。あらゆる方向を向き、人々のどんな苦難も見逃さないことを宣言している。穏やかで優しい顔をはじめ、怒ったり笑ったり、その表情はさまざまだ。東大寺二月堂（奈良）には、二尊の十一面観音像が祀られている。「お水取り」は、この秘仏（p.109）を前にすべての人類の罪を懺悔し、国家の安寧を祈る法要である。同じ奈良の長谷寺の本尊は、霊験あらたかな仏として著名。ふつうの十一面観音は水瓶や蓮華を手に蓮華座に立つが、長谷寺像は錫杖を持って岩をかたどった台座（p.107）に立っている。

Senju Kannon
(Sahasrabhuja)

Senju Kannon is given a thousand arms to complete the commitment to save all people by any means possible. *Senju Kannon* has an eye in each hand so that no entreaty is overlooked. The omnipotence of this *Kannon* is further represented by both the objects in its hands with which it performs its meritorious deeds, and the 11 heads with which it is crowned. Although many statues of *Senju Kannon* limit the number of arms to forty in addition to the main arms folded in prayer, there are statues that have actually been sculpted with a thousand arms. Examples include statues at *Tōshōdaiji* Temple (*Nara*) and *Fujiidera* Temple (*Osaka*), which attest to the skill possessed by their *busshi*. The ultimate arrangement, however, is found in *Myōhōin Sanjūsangendō* Temple (*Kyoto*, p. 121), where a seated *Senju Kannon* as the *honzon* is surrounded by one thousand standing statues of *Senju Kannon*.

千手観音

　千の手は、人々を救うために、あらゆる手段を尽くすという覚悟のあらわれ。手にはそれぞれ目が備わっており、どんな願いも見逃さない。功徳を示すさまざまな持物を手にし、加えて頭上には11の顔を戴く、最強の観音である。中央で合掌する手を除き40手に省略されることが多いが、唐招提寺（奈良）や葛井寺（大阪）には、実際に千の手をもつ彫像が現存し、仏師の高度な技を見ることができる。本尊の千手観音坐像を、さらに千体の千手観音立像が取り囲むのが、妙法院三十三間堂（京都、p.121）である。

Monju Bosatsu
(Mañjuśrī)

Monju Bosatsu leads people to enlightenment by means of wisdom. Born in India and a disciple of the historical Buddha, his discourse with *Yuimakoji* (Vimalakirti) is recorded in the Vimalakirti Sutra. *Monju Bosatsu* and *Yuimakoji* are represented by a pair of statues made in the 12th century and are now housed in *Tōkondō* Hall at *Kōfukuji* Temple (*Nara*). The popular proverb, "When three gather together, there is the wisdom of *Monju*" (similar in meaning to "Two heads are better than one"), which is based on an anecdotal account in the sutra, led to this statue becoming the object of prayers for academic accomplishment among the common classes. In the basic form, *Monju Bosatsu* statues carry the sword of wisdom and ride on the back of a *shishi* lion. The characteristic hairstyle is tied into five or six small buns. A Chinese grouping of *Monju* escorted by four disciples was transmitted to Japan. One such example, which is housed at *Monjuin* Temple (a.k.a. *Abe Monju, Nara*), was made by a mature *Kaikei*.

文殊菩薩
もんじゅ ぼ さつ

　智慧の力で、人々を悟りへと導く菩薩。インドに生まれた実在の人物で、維摩居士という論客と論争したことが経典に記される。興福寺（奈良）東金堂には、維摩と対になる12世紀の像が祀られている。知的な逸話が背景となって、「三人寄れば文殊の知恵」（みんなで知恵を絞れば良い考えが浮かぶ）という言葉も生まれ、庶民の間では学業成就が祈られるようになった。智慧の象徴である剣を手に、獅子の背に坐すのが基本のかたち。特徴的なのは髪型で、小さな髻（髪束）を5つも6つも結う像があり、独創的でかわいらしい。文殊が4人の眷属を引き連れる中国生まれの群像は日本にも伝わる。「安倍の文殊」と通称される奈良の文殊院では、快慶の円熟期の大作に会うことができる。

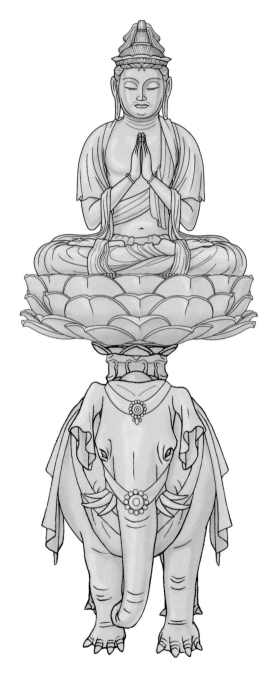

Fugen Bosatsu
(Samantabhadra)

With hands together in prayer and riding an elephant with six tusks, *Fugen Bosatsu* is dedicated to saving all sentient beings. *Fugen Bosatsu* combines the teachings and practice of Buddhism and is considered the Buddha of action. In early appearances, *Fugen Bosatsu* was paired with *Monju Bosatsu* and together they flanked *Shaka Nyorai*. The triad of *Shaka Nyorai* at the center with the combined wisdom of *Monju* and the practice of *Fugen* is one of the ideal representations in Buddhist statuary. The merits of *Fugen Bosatsu* are taught in the Lotus Sutra in relation to the final state of women, and for this reason this deity once attracted such fervent devotion from women of nobility that single statues were produced. *Fugen Bosatsu* also represents the virtue of longevity; therefore, in esoteric Buddhism *Fugen Bosatsu* developed into *Fugen Enmei* (Long Life) *Bosatsu*, who is typically portrayed with twenty arms and riding an elephant with three heads.

普賢菩薩

　　合掌し、6つの牙をもつ白象に乗ってどこにでも現れ、衆生を救う。教えと実践を兼ね備えた、行動する仏である。古くは、文殊菩薩とペアを組み、釈迦如来の脇を固めた。釈迦如来を中心に、智慧を司る文殊と行動する普賢が三尊をなすことは、仏教におけるひとつの理想の表現である。普賢菩薩の功徳を記す『法華経』は、女性の往生を説く。そのため、貴族の女性たちから熱烈な信仰を得て、独尊像がつくられるようになった。普賢菩薩には延命の徳もあり、密教では普賢延命菩薩という尊格に発展させた。こちらの像は腕が20本あったり、乗っている象の頭が3つあったりと、密教らしい造形を見せる。

Jizō Bosatsu
(Kṣitigarbha)

"Kṣitigarbha" in Sanskrit means "to hold the world within," and like the great earth, *Jizō Bosatsu* has an unwavering heart in the intention to save all sentient beings. *Jizō Bosatsu* vowed to lead all those in the Six Realms of Karmic Rebirth (the six worlds of heaven, humans, inhumans, animals, hungry spirits, and hell, where all beings live due to their own faults) into salvation. *Jizō Bosatsu*'s distinguishing features are a shaven head and robes similar to those of a monk, suggesting that there is no need for special attire when serving people. Devotion to this *bosatsu* spread among the common classes, and *Jizō Bosatsu* statues were made to grant various benefits, such as taking on a person's suffering, giving longevity, granting children to the barren, and easing the labor of childbirth. It is not unusual to see a *Jizō Bosatsu* statue enshrined at the side of a road, testifying to the fact that this deity has attracted great devotion and popularity in Japan.

地蔵菩薩

　サンスクリット語の名前は、大地を包蔵するという意味。大地のように揺るぎない心で、衆生を救済する仏である。地蔵菩薩は、六道（自らの行いのせいで生死をくり返す6つの世界、地獄、餓鬼、畜生、修羅、人、天）に輪廻して苦しむ人々を、ひとり残らず救済することを誓った。トレードマークは、菩薩では唯一の剃髪。僧侶と同じように、袈裟を着ける場合もある。人々に寄り添うのに、特別な装束は必要なかったのであろう。信仰は庶民の間で広がりをみせ、苦難の肩代わりや延命、子授けや安産など、さまざまな利益をもつ地蔵が生まれた。道端に祀られていることも珍しくない、日本ではもっとも親しまれている仏である。

Trivia

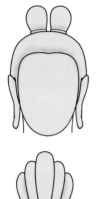

Zukō: around head

Hairstyles

Hair is carefully arranged high on top of the head in various styles.

Aureoles

Background decorations representing the hallowed light released by a Buddha. (See *Kōhai*, p. 112)

Kyoshinkō: full body

●豆知識

髪型
菩薩の髪は長く、頭上に結い上げる。そのスタイルはバリエーションが豊富。

光背 (頭光、挙身光)
仏が尊い光を放っている様を意匠化したのが、光背。(p.112)

Lotus Pedestals

Lotus flowers grow out of the mud to bloom as beautiful flowers. As a symbol of purity, most *nyorai* and *bosatsu* are placed on lotus seats.

Gyorinbuki: fish scale pattern

Fukiyose: aligned in a vertical row

Attire

Long *tenne* shawl gives the statue an exotic Indian look.

蓮華座（魚鱗葺き、吹き寄せ）
泥のなかで美しい花を咲かせる蓮華は、穢れなきことの象徴。如来と菩薩のほとんどに蓮華座が用いられる。

装い
天衣という長いショールをまとうなど、インド風の装いが菩薩の特徴。

Chapter 4

Myō-ō
Statuary

第四章

明王部の仏像

The Vidyārajā Statues: *Butsuzō* of *Myō-ō*

Said to have been born from mantra, the sacred words that condense esoteric truth, these Wisdom Kings (*myō-ō* in Japanese), are mystical beings. Originating from an esoteric tradition, these enlightened beings are ranked after the *nyorai* and *bosatsu*.

Their most prominent characteristic is their wrathful facial expressions. The reason for these angry expressions, according to esoteric teaching, is that they will use any means, including threats and intimidation, to save those beings that have slipped through the hands of the *nyorai* and *bosatsu*. In other words, they are the last line of defense; the benevolence they offer is the last resort for the unsaved.

Many *myō-ō* statues are created with multiple faces, eyes, hands, and feet. They have a monstrous quality and as sculptures are difficult to render three-dimensionally. Information about these statues was most likely transmitted to Japan as two-dimensional diagrams from which three-dimensional *butsuzō* were carved.

These esoteric *butsuzō*, which stand in stark contrast to the serene and silent *nyorai* and feminine *bosatsu*, enrich the statuary of the Buddhist pantheon and infuse it with powerful energy.

明王部の仏像

　　密教の真理を凝縮した言葉である真言から生まれたとされる、神秘的な尊格。本来は出自を異にするが、如来と菩薩に次ぐ尊格となった。

　　最大の特徴は、怒りをあらわにした表情。なにゆえ忿怒の形相をするかといえば、如来と菩薩の救いの手から漏れた衆生を、恫喝してまで救おうとしているからだと密教では説く。いわば、最後の砦。あとのない、優しさである。

　　明王の多くは、複数の顔、目、手足をもつ。異形の姿であり、彫刻として造形化することは難しい。日本では、おそらく図像という平面の情報しかもたらされないなかで、立体の仏像が刻まれた。静の如来、女性的な表情と肉体をもつ菩薩とはまったく違う容姿をもつ密教の仏が加わり、仏教の造形はより豊かに、パワフルになった。

Fudō Myō-ō
(Acalanātha: Immovable One)
ふ どう みょう おう
不動明王

Seitaka Dōji
(Ceṭaka)
せい た か どう じ
制吒迦童子

Kongara Dōji
(Kiṃkara)
こん が ら どう じ
矜羯羅童子

Fudō Myō-ō
(Acalanātha: Immovable One)

In the esoteric Buddhist tradition, which considers *Dainichi Nyorai* to be the supreme Buddha, *Fudō Myō-ō* is *Dainichi Nyorai*'s incarnation or messenger. This makes it the principal deity among the *myō-ō* group of statues. *Fudō Myō-ō* is portrayed with wide-open, piercing eyes and a fiercely shut mouth that reveals fangs. Set against a *kaen*, a fiery aureola, it is an expression of total wrath. Not all people can be led to salvation with gentle discourse, and so the final recourse is to reveal a storm of rage.

Few *Fudō Myō-ō* statues are found in India and China, but in Japan they receive much devotion and are called *Ofudōsama*. This name reflects the widespread familiarity and popular veneration of *Fudō Myō-ō*. When *Kūkai* (p. 112) returned from China in 806, he brought with him the doctrines of esoteric Buddhism, and faithfully transmitted the teachings on *Fudō Myō-ō*. Since then, the belief in this deity has shown a development all its own. When arranged as a triad, *Fudō Myō-ō* is flanked by *Kongara Dōji* and *Seitaka Dōji*.

不動明王

　名前の意味は、「動かざる者」。密教において最高の存在である大日如来の、使いとも化身ともいわれる明王グループ最高位の仏である。両目をカッと見開き、噛みしめた口には牙もみえる。火焔をかたどった光背を背にし、怒りを全身で表現。優しく諭すだけでは救えない人々を、なおも救うために、最終手段として激しい怒りをあらわにする。

　不動明王はインドや中国では、わずかしか確認されていないが、日本では「お不動さま」として誰もが知る親しい存在。806年に唐から帰国した空海 (p.112) は、密教の教義をもたらし、そのなかで不動明王の存在を正確に紹介した。それを発端に、長い時間をかけて独自の発展をとげたのである。三尊となる場合は、矜羯羅と制吒迦の二童子を従える。

Fudō Myō-ō
(Acalamātha: Immovable One)
不動明王

Godai Myō-ō p. 60-65
(Five Great Wisdom Kings)

The *Godai Myō-ō* grouping is arranged with *Fudō Myō-ō* seated in the center surrounded by the four other wisdom kings (p. 16); *Gōzanze Myō-ō* (east), *Gundari Myō-ō* (south), *Daiitoku Myō-ō* (west), and *Kongōyasha Myō-ō* (north), who is replaced by *Ususama Myō-ō* in the *Tendai* school. Each of these statues manifests great wrath, and except for the central *Fudō Myō-ō*, they are all strange representations with multiple faces and arms. In all cases, they exhibit a terrifying appearance. The earliest known group of *Godai Myō-ō*, which has miraculously survived to today, was made for the *Tōji* (a.k.a. *Kyō-ōgokokuji*) Temple (*Kyoto*, p. 122).

五大明王 p.60-65
　不動明王坐像を中心に、降三世明王（東）・軍荼利明王（南）・大威徳明王（西）・金剛夜叉明王（天台宗では烏枢沙摩明王、北）の四明王が四方を囲む (p.16)。これを、五大明王と呼ぶ。すべてが忿怒の表情を浮かべるのに加え、中央の不動明王を除く四方の明王は、複数の顔や手足をもつ異形の仏。いずれも、おどろおどろしい姿だ。日本に初めて五大明王がつくられたのは京都の東寺（教王護国寺　p.123）で、奇跡的に現存している。

Gōzanze Myō-ō
(Trilokavijaya: East)

Endowed with three faces
and standing on the Hindu
god Siva and his consort.

降三世明王（東）

　3つの顔をもち、ヒンドゥー教のシヴァ
神とその妃を踏みつける。

Gundari Myō-ō
(Kuṇḍalī: South)

Holding a coiled snake, the symbol of *bonnō* (destructive emotions).

軍荼利明王 (南)
　正しい判断を妨げる煩悩の象徴である
蛇を体に巻きつける。

Daiitoku Myō-ō
(Yamāntaka: West)

Possessing six faces, arms, legs and
riding on a buffalo.

大威徳明王 (西)

　顔・腕・足を6つずつもち、水牛に乗
っている。

Kongōyasha Myō-ō
(Vajrayakṣa: North)

Turning its five-eyed face to the front.

こんごう や しゃみょうおう
金剛夜叉明王（北）
目を5つもつ顔を正面に向ける。

Aizen Myō-ō

(Rāgarāja)

In Sanskrit, Rāgarāja means "King of Sexual Passion," which refers to the ability of *Aizen Myō-ō* to purify sensual lust, the most difficult *bonnō* to overcome. The means to do this is not by negating strong desire, but to turn the power back on itself. This is based on the teaching that even in a state of ignorance it is possible to use forces of desire to gain enlightenment. In Japan, *Aizen Myō-ō* is prayed to for harmony and friendship. *Aizen Myō-ō* is portrayed with a bright red body and three eyes, which accent a raging appearance, and a crown resembling a *shishigashira* (lion's head) resting upon standing hair. *Aizen Myō-ō* has six hands that can hold various articles, but there is always a bow and arrow. *Aizen Myō-ō* resembles Eros and Cupid in Greco-Roman mythology, and some statues are posed drawing the bow to release an arrow into heaven. There is a legend about the *Aizen Myō-ō honzon* enshrined in *Aizendō* Hall at *Saidaiji* Temple (*Nara*, p.123) in the 13th century that says that during the Mongolian invasion of Japan, the *honzon* shot an arrow from the temple that caused the enemy to surrender.

愛染明王

　サンスクリット語では「愛欲の王」。煩悩のなかでも断ち切るのが難しい愛欲でさえ、浄化する仏だ。欲望を断つのではなく、その強さを逆に利用。迷いのまま、悟りへといたる力に変えるという教えが背景にある。日本では主に、和合や親睦が祈られた。真っ赤な体躯、3つの目をもつ忿怒の形相、逆立つ髪には獅子頭をかたどった冠をのせる。6本の腕がさまざまな持物を手にするが、かならず持つのは弓と矢。ギリシャ・ローマ神話のエロスやキューピッドを想像させる、弓を天に向けて射ようとするポーズをとる像もある。西大寺（奈良、p.123）愛染堂の本尊は、13世紀の制作。蒙古襲来のとき、一矢を放って敵を降伏させたとの伝承がある。

Trivia

Hairstyles

The hair of *Fudō Myō-ō* can be either straight or curled. Straight hair is from an earlier period.

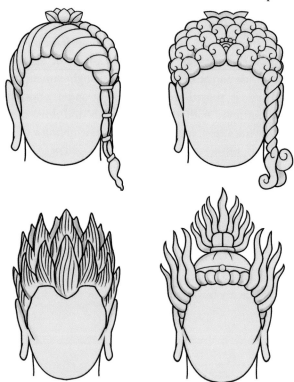

Representations of anger are seen in flame motif hairstyles called *Enpatsu*.

●豆知識

髪型

不動明王はおさげ髪が特徴。直毛と巻毛があり、直毛のほうが時代が古い。

不動明王以外の明王は、髪型でも怒りを表現。それを焔髪という。

Fiery Aureole

A radiant background of a flaming inferno reveals divine wrath.

Staggered Lotus Pedestals

Filled with vibrant energy, the *myō-ō* takes its stance with each foot firmly placed on small lotus flowers.

火焔光
燃え盛る炎をかたどった光背は、強い怒りのあらわれ。

踏割蓮華座
躍動感のある明王は、片足ずつ小さな蓮華を踏む。

Chapter 5

Ten
Statuary

第五章

天部の仏像

The Deva Statues: *Butsuzō* of *Ten*

The Deva (*ten* in Japanese) divinities were established when they were assimilated into the Buddhist pantheon from Brahmanism and Hinduism. They are heavenly deities serving as the major guardians of Buddha's Law. There are two types of *ten*: *Gohōshin*, who stand guard for the Buddhas and extend their protection to the faithful followers of Buddhism, and *Fukutokushin*, who bring happiness to people. Unlike *nyorai* and *bosatsu* who have set themselves the grand objective to save all of humankind, the *ten* take a stance much closer to that of sentient beings.

The *ten* group includes not only the supreme Hindu gods but also demons who, according to legend, have attained Buddhist enlightenment. For this reason, there are many more *ten* than there are *nyorai*, *bosatsu*, and *myō-ō*. The *ten* deities have various characteristics and appearances; they include deities of high birth, warriors clad in armor, half-human half-animal bodies and barefooted demonic spirits.

In the worship hall, *ten* statues are combined as guardians to protect the *honzon* that is the focus of worship. They are enshrined along the outer boundaries of the hall where they perform their defensive duties and provide visible movement to the spatial arrangement to bring out the aura of the *honzon*.

天部の仏像

　仏教がバラモン教やヒンドゥー教の神々を迎え入れて成立した尊格で、広く仏法を守護する役割を担っている。仏のみならず仏教を信仰する人々をも護る護法神と、人々を幸福へと導く福徳神という、大きくふたつに役割が分かれる。人々を救済するという大いなる目標を掲げる如来や菩薩と異なり、天部の仏はより人間に近いスタンスをとる。

　ヒンドゥー教の最高位だった神がいるかと思えば、悪鬼の類も仏教に教化されたという物語が加えられ、天部の仏として組み入れられた。そのため、如来や菩薩、明王に比べてはるかに数が多く、性格や姿かたちもさまざま。身分の高い俗人、甲冑に身を固めた武人、半人半獣や裸足の鬼神もいる。

　武装する天部像の多くは、チームを組んで本尊を守護する。堂内ではもっとも外側に安置されるが、本尊を護りながら見た目では動きをもたらし、引き立てている。

Bonten
(Brahmā)
ぼんてん
梵天

Taishakuten

(Indra)

<ruby>帝<rt>たい</rt>釈<rt>しゃく</rt>天<rt>てん</rt></ruby>

Bonten p. 74
(Brahmā)

Originally the Creator of the Universe in ancient Indian Brahmanism, *Bonten* was later incorporated into the Buddhist pantheon as the highest deity in the *ten* group. Often paired with *Taishakuten*, *Bonten* is positioned standing guard on the flanks of *nyorai* and *bosatsu*. While in many statues and images *Bonten* appears dressed as a Chinese nobleman, in esoteric Buddhism, as shown in the illustration, *Bonten* appears with multiple faces and several arms, wearing adornments similar to those found on statues of *bosatsu*, and sitting on a dais supported by geese.

Taishakuten p. 75
(Indra)

Taishakuten originated from the god Indra, who in ancient Indian tradition was victorious over the asuras. He is often found standing guard on the flank of a *nyorai* and *bosatsu*. When paired with *Bonten*, he is identified as a god of war by the armor he wears. In esoteric Buddhism, he sits on a white elephant.

梵天 p.74
　古代インドのバラモン教で、宇宙の創造神として君臨したブラフマー神が、梵天の前身。天部グループの最高位として仏教に迎えられたが、もっぱら帝釈天とペアを組み、如来や菩薩の脇を固める。中国の貴人のような姿の像が多いが、密教における梵天像は、イラストのように複数の顔と腕をもち、菩薩と同じ装束を身に着け、鷲鳥をかたどった台座に座っている。

帝釈天 p.75
　帝釈天のルーツは、古代インドでアシュラと戦って勝利したというインドラ。梵天とともに、如来・菩薩の脇を固めることが多い。梵天と帝釈天がペアでつくられる場合、甲冑を

Kongō Rikishi
(Vajradhara)

First to meet worshippers at the gates of temples are the two protective *Kongō Rikishi* statues. They are often called *Niō*. *Kongō* refers to the weapon, *kongōsho*, that they hold in their hands and with which they greet all enemies of Buddha's Law that try to pass through the gates. Their upper bodies and feet are bare and they are endowed with powerful, muscular bodies that intimidate enemies. The pair comprises an *Agyō* statue, which has an open mouth, and an *Ungyō* statue, which has a closed mouth. Together they symbolize the beginning and end of all things.

身に着けて武勇神であることを示す一尊が、帝釈天である。密教では、白象に乗る坐像としてつくられる。

金剛力士 p.78-79

　寺院の門に安置され、参詣者を最初に迎える二尊は、仁王あるいは二王と呼ばれることも多い。金剛とは、手にする金剛杵という武器のこと。これを手に、門から侵入しようとする仏法の敵を最前線で迎え撃つ。裸形で裸足。隆々とした筋肉をもつ肉体を誇示し、敵を威嚇する。ものごとの始まりと終わりを象徴する、口を開ける阿形と閉じる吽形で、一対となる。

Agyō
(A: open mouth)
あ ぎょう
阿形

Ungyō
(Hūṃ: closed mouth)
うんぎょう
吽形

Shitennō p. 81-84
(Four Guardian Kings)

Dressed as warriors in armor, these four statues crush underfoot demonic creatures symbolizing evil. Placed at the four corners of a worship hall, they provide protection in the four directions (p. 14); *Jikokuten* (east), *Zōchōten* (south), *Kōmokuten* (west), and *Tamonten* (north). The *Shitennō* serve all types of *nyorai* and *bosatsu* as guardians of Buddhism. They are the earliest recorded statuary of guardian deities in Japan.

Bishamonten p. 85
(Vaiśravaṇa)

At times, *Tamonten,* one of the *Shitennō*, is worshipped independently, in which case his name is changed to *Bishamonten*. As the guardian of the northern realm, his power as *Tamonten* is further emphasized. *Bishamonten* receives great devotion as a warrior god. Usually, *Bishamonten* is shown standing on defeated demons, but there is a variant form called the *Tobatsu Bishamonten* where he is standing on a goddess figure.

四天王 p.81-84
甲冑を身に着けて武装し、悪の象徴である邪鬼を踏みつけて立つ持国天（東）、増長天（南）、広目天（西）、多聞天（北）は、堂宇の四隅に安置され東西南北を護る (p.14)。仏教守護のために、どんな如来・菩薩にも仕える。日本に仏教が伝来したのち、もっとも古くから造立された守護神である。

毘沙門天 p.85
四天王の一員である多聞天は、単独で祀られる場合がある。そのとき、多聞天は毘沙門天と名を変える。北方の守護という多聞天の役目をさらに強化した尊格で、武神として信仰を集めた。ふつうは鬼を踏みつけるが、女神を踏みつける兜跋毘沙門天という異形像がある。

Jikokuten
(Dhṛtarāṣṭra: East)

Henchman under
Taishakuten's order.

持国天（東）
帝釈天直属の部下。

Zōchōten

(Virūḍhaka: South)

Commander
overpowers demons.

Kōmokuten

(Virūpākṣa: West)

Representing wisdom by
holding a brush and sutra
while in full armor.

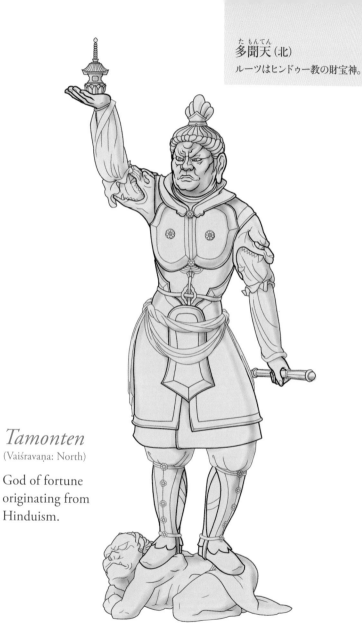

Tamonten
(Vaiśravaṇa: North)

God of fortune
originating from
Hinduism.

Bishamonten

(Vaiśravaṇa)

When *Tamonten* is
worshipped
independently,
he becomes
Bishamonten.

Jūnishinshō p. 87-92
(Twelve Heavenly Generals)

The *Jūnishinshō* are twelve guardian deities specially grouped to protect *Yakushi Nyorai*. Each deity is clad in armor and holds a weapon. The number twelve is significant in that they provide protection for the twelve periods of time, the twelve directions, and the twelve *eto* (twelve earthly branches). Each deity is given a different pose, ranging from exaggerated movement to restraint, and the contrast of stillness and movement creates harmony.

十二神将 p.87-92
　薬師如来を護るために集結したガードマン・チーム。それぞれが甲冑を身に着け、武器を手にする。十二神ということから、12をサイクルとする時刻や方位、干支を護る存在ともなっている。派手な動きと抑制、静と動という異なるポーズをとる12体がつくられ、調和が目指される群像である。

Kubira
(Kumbhīra)
くびら
宮毘羅

Basara
(Vajra)
ばさら
伐折羅

Anchira
(Andira)
あんちら
安底羅

Mekira
(Mihira)
めきら
迷企羅

Sanchira
(Śaṇḍila)
さんちら
珊底羅

Anira
(Majira)
あにら
頞儞羅

Haira
(Pajra)
は　い　ら
波夷羅

Indara
(Indra)
いん　だ　ら
因達羅

90

Shindara
(Sindūra)
しん だ ら
真達羅

Makora
(Makura)
ま こ ら
摩虎羅

91

Shōtora

(Catura)

しょう と ら
招杜羅

Bikara

(Vikarāla)

び か ら
毘羯羅

Kichijōten p. 94
(Mahāśrī)

Among the deities in the *ten* group, there are those whose gender is clearly identifiable. *Kichijōten* is the Hindu goddess of beauty and prosperity and therefore is most clearly female. After her incorporation into Buddhism, her power to provide wealth and protect the faithful from disaster earned her many devotees. In many of her statues she is dressed as a Chinese noblewoman.

Benzaiten p. 95
(Sarasvatī)

The goddess of the sacred river in early Indian tradition became *Benzaiten* in Buddhism. In Japan, she was first depicted as a goddess holding weapons, who fought to protect Buddha's Law, but eventually her character as the goddess of music was emphasized and many statues were made with her playing a *biwa* (lute). Because of her original association with water, she is enshrined near the seashore at *Itsukushima* (*Hiroshima*) and *Enoshima* (*Kanagawa*), where she has gathered much devotion. *Benzaiten* is also one of the *Shichifukujin*, the Seven Lucky Gods who bestow good fortune.

きちじょうてん
吉祥天 p.94
　天部には、性別が明らかな尊格が含まれている。吉祥天はその筆頭で、ヒンドゥー教では美と繁栄の女神だった。仏教に再編されてからも財宝を授ける、災いを除く尊格として存在感を発揮。中国の貴婦人をモデルにつくられている像が多い。

べんざいてん
弁才天 p.95
　古代インドに流れていた聖なる河の女神が、弁才天となった。日本では武器を持って仏法を護る、戦う女神としてつくられたが、次第に音楽神という性格が強調され、琵琶を抱える像がつくられるようになった。河の神というルーツのままに、厳島（広島）や江ノ島（神奈川）など水辺に祀られる例が多く、いずれも深い信仰を集めた。福徳をもたらす七神「七福神」にも再編されている。

Kichijōten
(Mahāśrī)
きちじょうてん
吉祥天

Benzaiten
(Sarasvatī)
べんざいてん
弁才天

Hachibushū p. 97-100

(Eight Legions)

Among the gods of other religions who gave devotion to Buddha, these eight legions specifically pledged loyalty to *Shaka Nyorai*. In ancient India, these were considered to be demons and evil monsters. *Hachibu*, meaning "eight tribes," indicates the group consists of one god from each of the tribes. It is a group of deities gathered solely for the protection of *Shaka Nyorai*, and therefore without him they would not exist. In the past, enshrining a grouping of *Hachibushū* statues surrounding *Shaka Nyorai* would have required considerable wealth as well as a significantly large space. At *Kōfukuji* Temple (*Nara*, p. 124), one can find *Hachibushū* statues that were made using the *kanshitsu* (dry lacquer) technique.

八部衆 p.97-100
　仏に帰依した異教の神のなかで、釈迦如来に忠誠を誓った八神である。かつて古代インドでは鬼神、悪神の類だった。八部とは八つの部族を意味し、各部族から一神が参加して編成されている。釈迦を護るためだけに結集したチームであり、釈迦像がなければ、存在しえない宿命をもつ。釈迦が八部衆を引き連れる群像を安置するには、莫大な制作費用がかかることに加え、安置するスペースが必要となる。そうした造立への高いハードルをクリアしたのが、興福寺（奈良、p.125）に現存する八軀の乾漆像だ。

Gobujō
(Deva)
ごぶじょう
五部浄

Shakara
(Nāga)
しゃがら
沙羯羅

Hibakara
(Mahoraga)
ひばから
畢婆迦羅

Kubanda
(Yakusa)
くばんだ
鳩槃荼

Karura
(Garuḍa)
かるら
迦楼羅

Kendatsuba
(Gandharva)
けんだつば
乾闥婆

Ashura
(Asura)
あしゅら
阿修羅

Kinnara
(Kiṃnara)
きんなら
緊那羅

Nijūhachibushū (Twenty-Eight Legions)

This is a large grouping of statues gathered to protect *Senju Kannon*. The group contains not only warrior deities but also gods unrelated to combat such as musicians and even a fleshless being, clearly sending the message that protection is not only about martial prowess. The large *Nijūhachibushū* grouping includes *Bonten* and *Taishakuten* from the highest realms, as well as members of other groups such as *Ashura*, and as such, the *Nijūhachibushū* comprises unique and diverse statuary from the *ten* group.

Hachidaidōji (Eight Youthful Attendants)

These eight youthful attendants act in accordance with the orders of *Fudō Myō-ō*. Although *Fudō Myō-ō* can often be found in arrangements with two youthful attendants (p. 58), other statues of *Hachidaidōji* are very rare. One exceptional *Hachidaidōji* arrangement can be found at *Kongōbuji* Temple on Mount *Kōya* (*Wakayama*, p. 124).

二十八部衆

　　千手観音を護るためだけに、結集した集団。守護という役目を果たす武装神ばかりでなく、戦闘とはおよそ無縁の楽器を持つ神や、痩せさらばえた老人などが加わっており、護るとは武力だけではないという意味を伝えているようだ。二十八部衆という大所帯は、梵天や帝釈天という最高位の天部のほか、阿修羅など他のチームに加わっている尊格も含まれ、天部のオールスターといった趣である。

八大童子

　　不動明王の命を受けて行動する8人の少年グループ。不動明王は、二童子を連れた三尊をなすことが多く(p.58)、八大童子の作例は数少ない。そのなかで、高野山金剛峯寺(和歌山、p.125)の彫像は貴重である。

Trivia

Attire

Noble *ten* are adorned with the official garments of a Chinese aristocrats.

●豆知識

装い

中国の貴人の正装をするのが貴顕天部。
甲冑に身を固めるのが武装天部(右頁)。

持物(宝剣、戟)

武装天部はさまざまな武器を持つ。先端が3つに分かれる戟は「貪り・怒り・愚かさ」の3つの毒に立ち向かうもの。

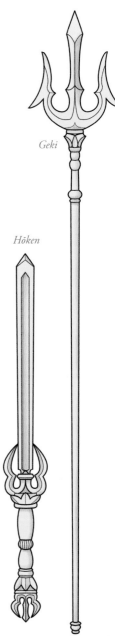

Geki

Hōken

Armor and Weapons

Warrior *ten* are dressed in full armor and
hold various weapons. *Geki* is meant to
combat the three poisons of greed, anger,
and foolishness.

Glossary

Treasured Statues

付録

用語集
訪ねてみたい仏像

Glossary | 用語集

Busshi

A sculptor specializing in Buddhist statuary. Painters of Buddhist sacred art are called *ebusshi*. In early Buddhist history, both types of artisans are thought to have been members of Buddhist orders.

仏師 ぶっし

仏像を専門に刻む彫刻家。仏画を手がける画家は、絵仏師と呼ぶ。古い時代には、どちらも僧籍にあったと考えられている。

Butsuga

The sacred paintings and pictures depicting Buddhas, which in the broadest sense include mandala (p. 113) and all other Buddhist sacred pictures.

仏画 ぶつが

仏の姿を描いた絵画。彫像に対して、画像と呼ぶ。広くは、曼荼羅(p.113)なども含む仏教絵画全般を意味する。

Chihōbutsu

Generally referring to statues made during the 8th to 10th century outside of the cultural sphere of Japan's early capitals of *Nara* and *Kyoto*. In addition to the formal statuary produced by the trained *busshi* (see above) working in the capital, many other less formal statues were created, which is testimony to the wide diffusion of Buddhism in Japan.

地方仏 ちほうぶつ

主に8〜10世紀に都がおかれた奈良と京都およびその文化圏以外の土地でつくられた仏像をいう。都の専門仏師(上段参照)とはまったく違う作風の仏像が、数多く生まれている。日本で仏教が、いかに浸透したかを物語る。

Daibutsu

The standard height for a Buddhist statue is 4.8 meters, which, according to the scriptures, was Buddha's height. Any statue taller than this is called a *daibutsu.* The *Nara Daibutsu,* seated *Rushanabutsu* at *Tōdaiji* Temple (*Nara,* p. 118), was made in the 8th century by Emperor *Shōmu* to establish his rule over the country. There have been other cases where leaders have ordered the creation of large statues to show their political power; however, the reasons behind the making of the regionally well-known *Kamakura Daibutsu,* seated *Amida Nyorai* at *Kōtokuin* Temple (*Kanagawa*), remain unknown.

Daiza

The pedestals that statues stand or sit upon. An example is the lotus-shaped dais, which is reserved for enthroning the highest-ranking *butsuzō* and cannot be used for statues from the *ten* group of deities. Various rules are applied to each group of statues.

大仏 だいぶつ

仏像をつくるとき、経典が仏の等身と説く一丈六尺(約4.8メートル)という像高がひとつの基準となっている。これを超えたものを一般に大仏と呼ぶ。現存する「奈良の大仏」(p.119 盧舎那仏坐像、東大寺、奈良)は、8世紀に聖武天皇が国を治めるために造立したものだが、時の権力者が自らの力を示すために造立する場合もあった。関東では著名な「鎌倉の大仏」(阿弥陀如来坐像、高徳院、神奈川)は、つくられた経緯はまったくわかっていない。

台座 だいざ

仏像が坐す、あるいは立つところ。さまざまな種類があり、代表的な蓮華をかたどった台座は格式が高く、天部のグループは使用できないなど、尊格に応じた決まりがある。

Enmaō

The god of hell originating in Indian mythology, in Sanskrit "Yamaraja." He is widely known in popular Buddhist belief as a judge of the dead in the underworld. His imagery is characterized by fierce, angry features.

Ganjin (688–763)

The Chinese monk who upon invitation eventually brought the teachings of the *Risshū* school of Buddhism to Japan. After five unsuccessful attempts he finally arrived in Japan, but because of his travail he had become blind. He established the first ordination platform in Japan at *Tōdaiji* Temple (*Nara*), making it possible to take vows and be ordained without going to China. In 759, he founded the *Tōshōdaiji* Temple (*Nara*) where he later passed away. A statue of *Ganjin* made in the 8th century is considered the oldest statue made of a great monk, and is an unsurpassed masterpiece.

閻魔王 えんまおう
インドを起源とする地獄の王。冥界で死者を裁く存在として、広く庶民に知られている。激しい怒りの表情が特徴である。

鑑真 がんじん
(688 ～ 763)
律宗を伝えるため、日本からの要請を受け来日した中国の高僧。5回の失敗を経て、ようやく来日したときには、失明していたという。東大寺(奈良)に日本に初めて戒壇(戒を授ける場所)を設け、これにより中国に赴かなくても戒を受けることが可能になった。759年に唐招提寺(奈良)を創立し、この地で没した。8世紀に制作された鑑真和上像は、日本の肖像彫刻の始まりにして最高傑作。

Gyokugan

A method for fashioning the eyes of a wooden statue using shiny crystal stones to mimic the human eye. The technique was developed in the 12th century when artisans wanted to give their sculptures more realistic features.

Hibutsu

Special Buddhist statues that normally remain hidden and are not put on display. Whereas some *hibutsu* are never exposed to the public, others are brought out or their altars are opened on specific days of the year for worshippers to visit. When a statue is exposed for worship, it is referred to as *kaichō* or *kaihi* (unveiling). In many cases, a surrogate statue known as the *omaedachi* is enshrined.

玉眼 ぎょくがん

水晶を使って、人間の目に近い光を表現する、木彫像に用いられる技法。写実を目指した12世紀に生みだされた。

秘仏 ひぶつ

通常は拝観が許されない仏像。絶対に公開されないものから、月日を定めて公開されるものまで、さまざま。公開されるときは、仏を納めた厨子の扉を開くという意味で、「開帳」や「開扉」と呼ぶ。ふつうは拝めない秘仏に代わり、「お前立ち」という分身を安置することがある。

Inzō

The roles and characteristics of the Buddhist pantheon are expressed in the poses of the individual statues. *Inzō*, "mudra" in Sanskrit, are hand and finger gestures that have symbolic meanings. The *semui-in* mudra, formed with the hand raised with palm facing out, and the *yogan-in* mudra, formed with the hand extended downward with palm facing up, are often combined to mean, respectively, "fear not" and "your wish will be granted." The *zenjō-in* mudra (p. 32) used to represent the Buddha in meditation is also the mudra taken when a practitioner meditates.

Jimotsu

The various objects and paraphernalia held in the hands of a statue. These can be religious objects, precious treasures, weapons, musical instruments, or plants. An example is the *suibyō* (water jar) often held by *Kannon Bosatsu* that contains the sacred water used to wash away spiritual impurities. Another example is the various weapons held by the statues in the *ten* group, whose role is to protect Buddha's Law. These are

印相 いんぞう

仏像は自らの役割や性格を姿かたちで示すが、手や指のかたちのことを印相という。よくみられるのは、掌を前に向けて上げる施無畏印と、掌をみせて下げる与願印の組み合わせ。施無畏印は「恐れることはない」、与願印には「願いはすべてかなえる」という意味がある。釈迦が瞑想する姿をルーツとする禅定印(p.32)は、座禅を組むときにも結ぶ。

持物 じもつ

仏像が手にする持ち物のことで、法具・宝物・武器・楽器・植物など多種多様。観音菩薩は穢れを祓う霊水が入っている水瓶、仏法を守護する役割を担う天部は武器を持つなど、力や役目を象徴する。

important symbols representing the strength and functions of each particular statue.

Jōchō (?–1057)

A *busshi* (p. 106) with a balanced, elegant style that was appreciated by the nobility of his time. His style became a lasting standard for sculpting Buddhist statues. The only extant work of his is the seated *Amida Nyorai* in *Byōdō-in* Temple (*Kyoto*, p. 119); however, there are many statues today that were made by other *busshi* following in his tradition. He is also the master sculptor who developed *yosegizukuri* (p. 19), a method of joining various carved parts to make a wooden statue.

Kaikei

A *busshi* (p. 106) active in the 13th century thought to have been a disciple of *Unkei's* (p. 117) father. He was influenced by the Chinese Song-period style of statuary and established a refined, elegant style of his own. This style is referred to as "*Annamiyō*" and was influential for a long period of time.

定朝 じょうちょう
(？〜 1057)

穏健で優美な仏を刻んだ仏師(p.106)。その作風は、当時の貴族の好みにあい、長きにわたり仏像を造立する際の基本となった。平等院の本尊(p.119 阿弥陀如来坐像、京都)が唯一の現存作例だが、その作風を踏襲した他の仏師の作品は数多く残されている。複数の木材を組み合わせてつくる、「寄木造り」(p.19)を考えだした仏師でもある。

快慶 かいけい
(生没年不詳)

13世紀を中心に活躍した仏師(p.106)。運慶(p.117)の父の弟子と考えられている。中国・宋の作風に影響を受け、優美な作風を確立。「安阿弥様(あんなみよう)」と呼ばれた作風は、長く影響を与えた。

Kirikane

A decorative technique of cutting gold leaf into various patterns. Introduced from China, it was first used on Buddhist statues in Japan in the 8th century. This method of gilding was thought to provide statues with a degree of splendor and was later widely adopted by other crafts and pictorial art.

截（切）金 きりかね

金箔を線状に裁断し、文様をあらわす繊細な技法。中国から伝わり、日本では8世紀の仏像に確認されている。仏像の荘厳から始まって、工芸や絵画にも用いられるようになった。

Kōhai

A representation of the light emitted by a Buddha. These ornamentations are positioned behind a statue to provide a sublime atmosphere. There are various designs of aureole that are used to express the individual nature of the deity depicted. For example, for a Buddha with a fierce countenance, flame designs are used (p. 69).

光背 こうはい

仏は光を放つ存在であるということを、造形化したもの。仏像の背後に据えて、仏を荘厳する。忿怒の表情を浮かべる仏には、炎をかたどった火焔光背（p.69）といったように、尊格の性格を反映した意匠が施される。

Kūkai

(a.k.a. Kōbō Daishi, 774–835)

Established Shingon school and founded the temple complex on Mount Kōya in Wakayama, Japan. He went to China in the Tang period to study esoteric Buddhism, which had only entered Japan in part, and after

空海 くうかい
（弘法大師 こうぼうだいし）
（774 ～ 835）

高野山（和歌山）を開いた真言宗の開祖。中国・唐で学び、それまで断片的にしか伝わっていなかった密教を、初めて体系的なものとして日本にもたらした。

his return he was the first to develop the teachings into a cohesive system.

Mandala

In Sanskrit, "mandala" means graphic images of true essence, and the true essence of the Buddhist world is conceptualized and systematically represented in these diagrams. They are employed most often in esoteric Buddhism in the *ryōkai mandala* (Mandala of the Two Realms, namely, the womb and the diamond), which depicts Buddhist cosmology with *Dainichi Nyorai* at the center. There are other mandala depicting the *jōdo* (pure land) with *Amida Nyorai* and other Buddhas, which are called the *jōdo mandala*.

Nehan

Nehan, "nirvana" in Sanskrit, is the state of bliss that Shākyamuni entered at his death. He did so lying on his side under a sal tree, and this is the way he is depicted in sculptures and *butsuga* (p. 106). In Japan, there are few examples of this type of statuary, but there are many pictorial representations called *nehanzu*. *Nehanzu* are hung at memorial services called *nehan-e*, which are conducted at many temples.

曼荼羅 まんだら
サンスクリット語の意味は「本質を図示したもの」。仏教世界の本質を理念的にとらえ、体系的に表現している。主に大日如来を中心とする密教世界を表わす、胎蔵界・金剛界の「両界曼荼羅」をいうが、阿弥陀如来など諸仏の浄土の様子を描いた絵画も、「浄土曼荼羅」と呼ばれる。

涅槃 ねはん
釈迦の入滅をいう。釈迦が沙羅双樹の下に横たわり入滅するさまは、彫刻でも絵画においても表現された。日本では彫像は少ないが、仏画（p.106）は数多い。涅槃図を掛けて釈迦を偲ぶ涅槃会という法要は、現在でも多くの寺院で催されている。

Saichō
(a.k.a. *Dengyō Daishi*, 767–822)

Founder of the *Tendai* school of Buddhism. After returning from studying Tiantai Buddhism in China during the Tang period, *Saicho* continued his practice of *Tendai* Buddhism on Mount *Hiei* in *Shiga*, Japan. He enshrined a statue of *Yakushi Nyorai* in his worship hall, which after his death became *Enryakuji* Temple and the center of the *Tendai* school of Buddhism.

Shinbutsushūgō

The eclectic beliefs that integrate indigenous Japanese deities, *kami*, with Buddhist teachings. After the arrival of Buddhism in Japan in the 6th century, shrines and temples were often integrated. Until the *Shinbutsuhanzenrei* (*kami* and Buddhas Separation Order) was enacted in 1868, it was quite normal to have small shrines on temple grounds and Buddhist statuary within shrine complexes.

最澄 さいちょう
(伝教大師 でんぎょうだいし)
(767 ～ 822)

中国・唐で天台教学を学び、日本に天台宗を開いた。修行を重ねた比叡山に薬師如来を安置した堂宇が、最澄の没後に延暦寺（滋賀）となり、天台宗の総本山となった。

神仏習合
しんぶつしゅうごう

日本の在来の神と、外国からもたらされた仏教が融合した思想。仏教が伝来した6世紀から、日本では神社と寺院が共存していた。1868年の神仏判然令の施行までは、寺院に祠があり、神社に仏像が祀られることはふつうだった。

Shinzō

Statues of *kami*, deities of Japan's indigenous religion (*Shintō*). Originally, the *kami* were not depicted or given any imagery, but with the arrival of Buddhist statuary in Japan, representations of these deities were produced. In contrast to *butsuzō*, which are made to be seen, *shinzō* are in principle hidden from view.

Shōtoku Taishi
(Prince *Shōtoku*, 574–622)

Son of Emperor *Yomei* who attempted to establish Buddhism as the principal system of belief of Japan. *Shōtoku Taishi* is also credited with the building of *Hōryūji* Temple (*Nara*) in the 7th century. For these reasons, he became a semi-legendary figure and many sculptures and pictures were made of him as objects of worship.

Shuji

The use of the Sanskrit letter of the name of a *nyorai* and *bosatsu* to represent them. *Shuji* can symbolize actual statues and they can be found in mandalas (p. 113).

神像 しんぞう
日本古来の宗教、いわゆる神道における神の像。本来、神は姿をもたないものだったが、仏像が伝来したことに影響を受け、造形化されるようになったと考えられている。仏像とは違い、基本的に目にすることはかなわない。

聖徳太子
しょうとくたいし (574～622)
仏教の精神をもって国を治めようとした用明天皇の皇子。7世紀に法隆寺(奈良)を創建した。その事績は半ば伝説化され、礼拝の対象となったことから多くの彫像や画像がつくられた。

種字 (子) しゅ(う)じ
如来・菩薩の名前を、サンスクリット語の1字であらわしたもの。尊像に代わるシンボル。種字だけで曼荼羅(p.113)もつくられた。

Tanjōbutsu

After Shākyamuni was born from the right side of his mother, Māyā, he took seven steps, raised his right hand to heaven, pointed to the earth with his left hand and said: "I am revered; the highest in heaven and on earth." Statues depicting this pose are venerated during the *kanbutsue* (a.k.a. *hanamatsuri*) festival held on April 8th to celebrate Shākyamuni's birth. Because *amacha* (sweat hydrangea tea) is poured on the head of the statue during the festival, these statues are made of gilt bronze.

Tori Busshi
(a.k.a. *Kuratsukuri no Tori*)

A *busshi* (p. 106) active at the beginning of the 7th century. His ancestors are said to have come from Liang in China during the Southern and Northern Dynasties period. He carved the *Shaka* Triad in *Kondō* Hall, *Hōryūji* Temple (*Nara*, p. 118), making him the first to produce orthodox Buddhist statues in Japan.

誕生仏 たんじょうぶつ

摩耶夫人の右腋から生まれた釈迦は、七歩進んで右手を上げて天を指し、左手は地を指して「天上天下唯我独尊（てんじょうてんげゆいがどくそん）」と唱えたという。その姿をあらわした仏像で、釈迦の誕生を祝う4月8日の灌仏会、通称「花祭り」の本尊となる。甘茶をかけて供養されることから、金銅仏がほとんど。

止利仏師 とりぶっし
（鞍作止利　くらつくりのとり）
（生没年不詳）

7世紀初めの仏師(p.106)。先祖は、中国・南朝の梁から渡来した人だという。法隆寺金堂の釈迦三尊像(p.119 奈良)を造像したことから、日本で初めて本格的な仏像をつくったとされている。

Unkei (?–1223)

A *busshi* (p. 106) active in *Nara*. He further developed the *yosegizukuri* technique (p. 19) of *Jochō* (p. 111) and organized his workshop based on the division of labor. In this way, he was able to meet the various demands placed on his work. His statues have a liveliness making him the representative carver of his time.

運慶 うんけい
(?～1223)
奈良を拠点に活躍した仏師(ぶっし)(p.106)。定朝(じょうちょう)(p.111) の生んだ「寄木造り」(よせぎづくり)(p.19) を進化させ、分業による工房を組織し、多様な需要に応えたと考えられる。生動感(せいどうかん)にあふれた仏像を生み、一時代を代表する。

Ten Treasured Statues of *Nyorai* to Visit

Shaka Triad

(bronze, 623, National Treasure),
Kondō Hall, *Hōryūji* Temple, *Nara.*

This statue was offered supplications for the recovery of *Shōtoku Taishi* (p.115) when he was ill. *Tori Busshi* (p.116) is the creator of this wonderful fusion of sculptural beauty and mystery.

Seated *Yakushi Nyorai*

(bronze, 7th or 8th century, National Treasure), *Kondō* Hall, *Yakushiji* Temple, *Nara.*

Given a solid body and settled securely in a seated position on its dais, the degree of refinement of this *nyorai* statue offers an ideal standard within the Buddhist statuary.

Seated *Rushanabutsu*

(bronze, 752, National Treasure), *Daibutsuden* Hall, *Tōdaiji* Temple, *Nara.*

After being burned and damaged by fire on several occasions, the head was repaired in the 17th century and the lotus petals on the pedestal were replaced in the 8th century, making it possible for this statue to survive to the present.

Standing *Nyorai*

(wood, 8th century, Important Cultural Property), *Shinhōzō* Gallery, *Tōshōdaiji* Temple, *Nara.*

Although this statue is headless, the beautiful, lightly carved robe reveals a body of well-rounded contours. Public viewing in spring and fall.

Standing *Yakushi Nyorai*

(wood, 8th century, National Treasure), *Jingoji* Temple, *Kyoto.*

With its stern expression and unusually powerful thighs, this statue has an unparalleled presence and force.

Standing *Yakushi Nyorai*

(wood, 8th century, National Treasure), *Gangōji* Temple, *Nara.*

A solid body creating a feeling of amplitude is wrapped in flowing robes, adding to the statue's standing presence. Entrusted to Nara National Museum.

Seated *Shaka Nyorai*

(wood, 9th century, National Treasure), *Mirokudō* Hall, *Murōji* Temple, *Nara.*

Seated in a relaxed manner, this statue is covered in a finely carved robe whose folds create beautifully flowing shading.

Seated *Yakushi Nyorai*

(wood, 9th century, National Treasure), *Shishikutsuji* Temple, *Osaka.*

Long lines of half-closed meditating eyes give an alluring quality to this attractive statue. It is well worth the climb to the hall at the top of the mountain to view this statue.

Seated *Amida Nyorai* (wood, 1053, National Treasure), *Hō-ōdō* Hall, *Byōdōin* Temple, *Kyoto*.

This statue's body, posture, and facial features are soft. People see beyond its dreaming gaze to the *gokurakujōdo* (blissful pure land).

Seated *Dainichi Nyorai* (wood, 1176, National Treasure), *Enjōji* Temple, *Nara*.

Representing the central Buddha in esoteric Buddhism, this statue gives the viewer the impression of youth. Although this is an early production by *Unkei* (p. 117), there is not one trace of faltering anywhere during its sculpting.

ぜひ訪ねてみたい【如来】十選

●法隆寺　金堂
釈迦三尊像（銅造、623年、国宝）奈良
聖徳太子（p.115）の病気平癒が祈られた仏。造形美と神秘性が融合した像の作者は止利仏師（p.116）である。

●薬師寺　金堂
薬師如来坐像（銅造、7または8世紀、国宝）奈良
充実した肉体をもち、坐す姿もゆるぎない。高い完成度は、仏像のひとつの理想形をみせる。

●東大寺　大仏殿
盧舎那仏坐像（銅造、752年、国宝）奈良
頭部は17世紀、台座の蓮弁は8世紀。焼失のつど再興されて、現在まで存在している。

●唐招提寺　新宝蔵
如来形立像（木造、8世紀、重文）奈良
豊かな肉体を感じさせる薄い衣の表現が美しい、頭部を欠く胴体。公開は春と秋のみ。

●神護寺
薬師如来立像（木造、8世紀、国宝）京都
険しい表情と、異常に張りつめた太腿。そこから生みだされる存在感と迫力は、比類がない。

●元興寺
薬師如来立像（木彫、8世紀、国宝）奈良
ボリュームある体躯を流麗な衣が包む、存在感にあふれた立ち姿。奈良国立博物館寄託。

●室生寺　弥勒堂
釈迦如来坐像（木造、9世紀、国宝）奈良
ゆったりと坐す仏がまとう衣には、細かい襞が刻まれ、陰影を見せつつ美しく流れる。

●獅子窟寺
薬師如来坐像（木造、9世紀、国宝）大阪
切れ長の目が一種のなまめかしさを醸す、魅力的な仏。山上に建つ堂宇まで、登る価値あり。

●平等院　鳳凰堂
阿弥陀如来坐像（木造、1053年、国宝）京都
体つきも構えも表情も、柔らかい。人々はこの夢見るような眼差しの先に、極楽浄土を見た。

●円成寺
大日如来坐像（木造、1176年、国宝）奈良
密教の教主でありながら、瑞々しい印象。若き運慶（p.117）の作だが、造形に破綻はみじんもない。

Ten Treasured Statues of *Bosatsu* to Visit

Standing *Kuse Kannon*

(wood, 7th century, National Treasure), *Yumedono* **Hall,** *Hōryūji* **Temple,** *Nara.*

This *hibutsu* is said to be the image of *Shōtoku Taishi*. There is undoubtedly a mysteriousness brought forth by the solid sculpting.

Seated *Miroku Bosatsu*

(wood, 7th century, National Treasure), *Reihōden* **Hall,** *Kōryūji* **Temple,** *Kyoto.*

This statue's clear features overflow with the deep compassion of a *bosatsu*. Similar statues extant on the Korean Peninsula testify to the active cultural exchange that took place in the past.

Seated *Bosatsu*

(wood, 7th century, National Treasure), *Chūgūji* **Temple,** *Nara.*

With its middle finger lightly touching its cheek, the meditative expression is as if caught in a dream. This statue has been meticulously carved from a single block of sacred wood.

Standing *Kumen Kannon*

(wood, 7th century, National Treasure), *Daihōzōin* **Hall,** *Hōryūji* **Temple,** *Nara.*

It is hard to believe that this detailed carving was done using a single block of sandalwood, but its unique presence and preciousness stands out far above the skilled craftsmanship.

Standing *Fukūkensaku Kannon*

(hollow dry lacquer, 8th century, National Treasure), *Hokkedō* **Hall (a.k.a.** *Sangatsudō*), *Tōdaiji* **Temple,** *Nara.*

A remarkably noble appearance created in a way that does not make one feel uncomfortable, despite its strange, eight-armed body. It is quite rare to find a halo of such grandeur.

Standing *Jūichimen Kannon*

(wood-core dry lacquer, 8th century, National Treasure), *Shōrinji* **Temple,** *Nara.*

With a bodyline filled with vitality, and its supple fingers, this statue is given movement. The far-reaching gaze leaves a long-lasting impression.

Standing *Jūichimen Kannon*

(wood, 9th century, National Treasure), *Hokkeji* **Temple,** *Nara.*

This sharply carved *Kannon* stands forth from its delicate lotus-shaped halo backing. Its beauty discourages anyone from approaching it casually.

Standing *Jūichimen Kannon*

(wood, 9th century, National Treasure), *Kōgenji* **Temple,** *Shiga.*

This statue's Indian features make it a rare type of statue in Japan. The superb carving skill has brought

forth a form that can only be
described as perfect.

Seated *Nyoirin Kannon*
**(wood, 9th century, National
Treasure)**, *Kanshinji* Temple, *Osaka*.
This plump, well-rounded statue,
which is made in keeping with the
esoteric Buddhist style, sits relaxed
and with an air of sensuality. Public
viewings are on April 17th and 18th
only.

Sentai Senju Kannon
**(wood, 1164, Important Cultural
Property)**, *Myōhōin Sanjūsangendō*
Temple (a.k.a. *Rengeōin*), *Kyoto*.
The *honzon* which is a National
Treasure, is surrounded by one
thousand more statues of *Senju
Kannon*. It is a miraculous spatial
depiction of a deep desire to bring
the world of Buddha into the reality
of this mundane life.

ぜひ訪ねてみたい【菩薩】10選

●法隆寺　夢殿
救世観音立像（木造、7世紀、国宝）奈良
聖徳太子を映したと伝わる秘仏。確かな造形に裏打ちされた容貌が醸すのは、神秘性である。

●広隆寺　霊宝殿
弥勒菩薩半跏像（木造、7世紀、国宝）京都
清楚な表情に菩薩の慈悲があふれる。朝鮮半島に似た像が現存し、活発な交流の証人でもある。

●中宮寺
菩薩半跏像（木造、7世紀、国宝）奈良
中指を頬にあて、思索にふける表情は夢見るよう。一本の霊木から丁寧につくられている。

●法隆寺　大宝蔵院
九面観音立像（木造、7世紀、国宝）奈良
一材の白檀から彫られたとは信じがたい精緻な彫技。それを超えて、仏像として存在する。

●東大寺　法華堂（三月堂）
不空羂索観音立像（脱活乾漆造、8世紀、国宝）奈良
8本の腕の異形を感じさせない端正な佇まいは出色。光背の精致なつくりも見事。

●聖林寺
十一面観音立像（木心乾漆造、8世紀、国宝）奈良
張りのある姿態に、しなやかな指が動きを与える。遠くを見るような眼差しも、印象的。

●法華寺
十一面観音立像（木彫、9世紀、国宝）奈良
蓮華をかたどった繊細な光背を背に、鋭い彫りの観音が立つ。その美しさは、近寄りがたい。

●向源寺
十一面観音立像（木造、9世紀、国宝）滋賀
佇まいは日本では珍しいインド風。優れた彫技が、非の打ちどころがない造形を生みだした。

●観心寺
如意輪観音坐像（木造、9世紀、国宝）大阪
豊満な体躯で、ゆったりと坐す姿が官能的な印象を醸す密教像。開扉は4月17・18日のみ。

●妙法院三十三間堂（蓮華王院）
千体千手観音立像（木造、1164年、重文）京都
本尊（国宝）を千体の立像が囲む。仏の世界を現世で得たいという願いが生んだ、奇跡的な空間。

Ten Treasured Statues of *Myō-ō* to Visit

Godai Myō-ō

(wood, 839, National Treasure),
Kōdō Hall, *Tōji* (a.k.a. *Kyō-ōgokokuji*)
Temple, *Kyoto*.

A production under the guidance of *Kūkai*, this group of five *Myō-ō* statues was the first of its kind made in Japan. Although their appearance is quite strange, they have a beauty all their own.

Godai Myō-ō

(wood, 10th century,
Important Cultural Property),
Daigoji Temple, *Kyoto*.

With its big eyes wide open in an unwavering stare, *Fudō Myō-ō* leads his company. Rather than feeling fear, one somehow senses a tinge of inherent humor.

Standing *Gundari Myō-ō*

(wood, 10th century, Important Cultural Property), *Nigatsudō* Hall, *Konshōji* Temple, *Shiga*.

This powerful statue stands almost four meters high and uniquely reflects the differences between the cultures of *Kyoto* and nearby *Shiga*.

Seated *Fudō Myō-ō*

(wood, 1005, Important Cultural Property), *Dōjuin* Temple, *Kyoto*.

Quietly enthroned but expressing its wrath, the Immovable One resides. This is one of the few temples where a person can have direct communion with a statue of this majesty.

Seated *Daiitoku Myō-ō*

(wood, 11th century,
Important Cultural Property),
Makiōdō Temple, *Oita*.

Even in *Kyushu*, far removed from the center of major statue production, this large sculpture with a demanding presence testifies to the transmission of formal carving techniques to the peripheral regions.

Fudō Myō-ō and *Nidōji*

(wood, 1186, Important
Cultural Property),
Ganjōjuin Temple, *Shizuoka*.

In this triad, *Fudō Myō-ō,* with its powerfully honed body, is flanked by two *dōji* attendants. It is a representative production in the *Kanto* area by *Unkei*.

Seated *Daiitoku Myō-ō*

(wood, 12th century, Important Cultural Property), *Ishibaji* Temple, *Shiga*.

Although classified as a "wrathful statue," it also conveys a peaceful calm. It was made as an independent statue and originally was the *honzon* used in the ceremonies of the *Tendai* school .

Seated *Fudō Myō-ō*

(stone, 12th century, Important Cultural Property), *Nissekiji* Temple, *Toyama*.

This is a dynamic representation carved on a large stone wall. This particular statue has gained the fervent devotion of followers of *Shugendō*, the old ascetic mountain religion of Japan.

Standing *Gōzanze Myō-ō*
(wood, 12th century, Important Cultural Property), *Myōtsūji* **Temple,** *Fukui.*

This majestic statue stands well over two meters. It is an independent, well-balanced icon that does not leave one with a feeling of discomfort, despite its eight arms.

Seated *Aizen Myō-ō*
(wood, 1247, Important Cultural Property), *Aizendō* **Hall,** *Saidaiji* **Temple,** *Nara.*

Sculpted by the unfailing and steady hand of *Zen-en busshi*, this *hibutsu* features bright coloration. Public viewing in spring and fall only.

ぜひ訪ねてみたい【明王】十選

●東寺 (教王護国寺) 講堂
五大明王像 (木造、839年、国宝) 京都
空海のプロデュースにより、日本で最初につくられた五尊像。異形ながら美しくもある。

●醍醐寺
五大明王像 (木造、10世紀、重文) 京都
巨大な目を見開いた不動明王が率いる群像は、恐ろしいというよりどこかユーモラスな趣き。

●金勝寺 二月堂
軍荼利明王立像 (木造、10世紀、重文) 滋賀
4メートルに迫る迫力満点の巨像。京都にほど近い地ながら、京都とは異なる文化が生んだ造形である。

●同聚院
不動明王坐像 (木造、1005年、重文) 京都
静かに坐して怒る姿は、まさに動かざる者。仏とじっくり対峙できる京都では数少ない寺院。

●真木大堂
大威徳明王坐像 (木造、11世紀、重文) 大分
都から離れた九州にも、都の正系仏師の技術が伝わっていたことを示す、存在感のある巨像。

●願成就院
不動明王及二童子像 (木造、1186年、重文) 静岡
鍛えられた肉体をもつ不動明王が、童子を従える三尊像。運慶の関東における代表作である。

●石馬寺
大威徳明王坐像 (木造、12世紀、重文) 滋賀
忿怒像ながら穏やかな印象。

独尊像としてつくられ、かつては天台修法の本尊だった。

●日石寺
不動明王坐像 (石造、12世紀、重文) 富山
巨大な岩壁に刻まれ、迫力満点。日本古来の山岳信仰、修験道の本尊として篤い信仰を集める。

●明通寺
降三世明王立像 (木造、12世紀、重文) 福井
2メートルをゆうに超える堂々たる像。8本の腕をもちながら違和感のない、整った独尊である。

●西大寺 愛染堂
愛染明王坐像 (木造、1247年、重文) 奈良
破綻のない造形と確かな彫技の作者は、善円。春と秋に公開される秘仏で、彩色も鮮やか。

Ten Treasured Statues of *Ten* to Visit

Standing *Shitennō*

(wood, 7th century, National Treasure), *Kondō* Hall, *Hōryūji* Temple, *Nara*.

While their facial expressions and stature are sublime, these four heavenly kings radiate a powerful presence. To be noted are the demon monsters underfoot with their unique characteristics.

Standing *Shitennō*

(dry lacquer, 7th century, Important Cultural Property), *Kondō* Hall, *Taimadera* Temple, *Nara*.

With his beard, this *Zōjōten* has exotic continental features. His facial expression allows a glimpse of the emotional conflict seething within and leaves a powerful impression on the heart of the viewer.

Standing *Shūkongōshin*

(clay, 8th century, National Treasure), *Hokkedō* Hall (a.k.a. *Sangatsudō*), *Tōdaiji* Temple, *Nara*.

Although this statue expresses overpowering fierceness and great rage, its armor adornment is covered in gorgeous colors. It is a *hibutsu* brought out for viewing only on December 16th.

Standing *Shitennō*

(clay, 8th century, National Treasure), *Kaidandō* Hall, *Tōdaiji* Temple, *Nara*.

These four statues strike various poses with beautifully proportioned bodies.

They are a wonderful example of a well-balanced group of statues.

Standing *Hachibushū*

(dry lacquer, 734, National Treasure), *Kokuhōkan* Gallery, *Kōfukuji* Temple, *Nara*.

Represented by the *Ashura* with its expression overflowing with sorrow, all eight statues take the appearance of youths, making this an unusual grouping of the *ten* type.

Standing *Tobatsu Bishamonten*

(wood, 8th century, National Treasure), *Hōmotsukan* Gallery, *Tōji* (a.k.a. *Kyō-ōgokokuji*) Temple, *Kyoto*.

Made in China during the Tang period. Clothed in a gown resembling armor, there is a gracefulness to this gallant young warrior from the exotic regions of western Asia.

Seated *Bonten* and *Taishakuten*

(wood, 839, National Treasure), *Kōdō* Hall, *Tōji* (a.k.a. *Kyō-ōgokokuji*) Temple, *Kyoto*.

These two statues stand in contrast to each other with the sensual aura of *Bonten* and the gallant features of *Taishakuten*. These are two of the earliest examples of statues in the *ten* category of esoteric Buddhist statuary found in Japan.

Standing *Hachidaidōji*

(wood, 12th century, National Treasure), *Kōyasan Reihōkan* Gallery, *Kongōbuji* Temple, *Wakayama*.

Lively force flows through the bodies of these winsome children figures. It is thought that it was *Unkei* who gave these statues their human-like expressions.

Standing *Kongōrikishi*
(wood, 1203, National Treasure), *Nandaimon* Gate, *Tōdaiji* Temple, *Nara*.

Although these giant statues stand over eight meters high, they were made in only 70 days. They stand as witness to the fact that efficiency and art are indeed compatible.

Standing *Kichijōten*
(wood, 1212, Important Cultural Property), *Jōruriji* Temple, *Kyoto*.

Female figures are rarely seen in Buddhist statuary. Her colorfully attractive attire is suited for this heavenly goddess.

ぜひ訪ねてみたい【天】十選

●法隆寺 金堂
四天王立像（木像、7世紀、国宝）奈良

表情も体軀も静的でありながら、圧倒的な存在感を放つ。足下の個性的な邪鬼にも注目。

●當麻寺 金堂
四天王立像（脱活乾漆造、7世紀、重文）奈良

髭をはやした増長天は、異国人の容貌。葛藤を抱えたかのような表情が心に残る。

●東大寺 法華堂（三月堂）
執金剛神立像（塑造、8世紀、国宝）奈良

圧倒的な忿怒の形相を見せつつ、甲冑には華麗な彩色が。12月16日のみ開扉される秘仏。

●東大寺 戒壇堂
四天王立像（塑造、8世紀、国宝）奈良

異なるポーズをとる美しいプロポーションの四軀が、見事な調和をみせる群像のお手本。

●興福寺 国宝館
八部衆像（脱活乾漆造、734年、国宝）奈良

憂いの表情を浮かべる阿修羅をはじめ、八尊すべてが少年の容貌をみせる群像は珍しい。

●東寺（教王護国寺）宝物館
兜跋毘沙門天立像（木造、8世紀、国宝）京都

中国・唐でつくられた像。ガウンのような甲冑をまとい、凛々しい西域の若者という趣だ。

●東寺（教王護国寺）講堂
梵天・帝釈天坐像（木造、839年、国宝）京都

官能的な梵天と、凛々しい帝釈天の一対は、密教の梵天・帝釈天像としては日本でもっとも古い。

●金剛峯寺 高野山霊宝館
八大童子像（木造、12世紀、国宝）和歌山

子供のような愛らしい体形に生気がみなぎる。人間に近い表現を求めた仏師は運慶と考えられる。

●東大寺 南大門
金剛力士立像（木造、1203年、国宝）奈良

8メートルを超える巨像だが、制作日数は約70日。効率と芸術は融合することを証明した。

●浄瑠璃寺
吉祥天立像（木造、1212年、重文）京都

女性天部ならではの、あでやかな装い。これほど女性らしい像は珍しい。

石井亜矢子　いしい・あやこ
和光大学芸術学科で
仏教美術・近世絵画史を学び、
美術専門紙記者を経てフリーランスに。
現在は仏教美術の調査研究に関わりつつ、
展覧会の企画や書籍制作、執筆活動など。
著書に『仏像の見方ハンドブック』(池田書店)、
『仏像図解新書』(小学館)ほか多数。

岩﨑　隼　いわさき・じゅん
マンガから水彩・油彩まで幅広く
手がけるイラストレーター。
実家は北海道小樽市の浄土真宗(三門徒派)専名寺。

装丁・本文デザイン
金田一亜弥(金田一デザイン)
英文翻訳
リングァ・ギルド

本書は小社刊『仏像図解新書』
(2010年発行)を再編集し、
英語訳を付けたものです。
日本語の表記は原則として
上記の新書にのっとり記載しています。
イラストは修正を加え
着色して掲載しています。

Bilingual Guide to Japan
BUDDHIST STATUARY

仏像バイリンガルガイド

2018年4月17日　初版　第2刷発行

著　者　石井亜矢子／岩﨑　隼
発行者　久保雅一

発行所　**株式会社小学館**
　　　　〒101-8001
　　　　東京都千代田区一ツ橋2-3-1
　　　　編集　03-3230-5563
　　　　販売　03-5281-3555
　　　　編集／矢野文子　販売／鈴木敦子

印刷所　**大日本印刷株式会社**
製本所　**株式会社若林製本工場**

©ISHII Ayako ／ IWASAKI Jun 2016 Printed in Japan
ISBN978-4-09-388460-0